Collins

Reimagine
Key Stage 3
Shakespeare

Imaginative ways to study Shakespeare in every year of KS3

Series editor: **Jo Heathcote**

Authors: **Hannah Appleton** and **Jo Heathcote**

William Collins' dream of knowledge for all began with the publication of his first book in 1819.

A self-educated mill worker, he not only enriched millions of lives, but also founded a flourishing publishing house. Today, staying true to this spirit, Collins books are packed with inspiration, innovation and practical expertise. They place you at the centre of a world of possibility and give you exactly what you need to explore it.

Collins. Freedom to teach

Published by Collins
An imprint of HarperCollins*Publishers*
The News Building, 1 London Bridge Street, London SE1 9GF

HarperCollins*Publishers*
1st Floor, Watermarque Building, Ringsend Road, Dublin 4, Ireland

Browse the complete Collins catalogue at
collinseducation.com

© HarperCollins*Publishers* Limited 2022

10 9 8 7 6 5 4 3 2 1

ISBN 978-0-00-855264-0

All rights reserved. No part of this publication may be reproduced, stored in a retrieval system, or transmitted in any form by any means, electronic, mechanical, photocopying, recording or otherwise, without the prior written permission of the Publisher or a licence permitting restricted copying in the United Kingdom issued by the Copyright Licensing Agency Ltd, 5th Floor, Shackleton House, 4 Battle Bridge Lane, London SE1 2HX.

British Library Cataloguing-in-Publication Data
A catalogue record for this publication is available from the British Library.

We would like to thank Thishani Wijesinghe for reviewing the resources in development.

Series editor: Jo Heathcote
Authors: Hannah Appleton and Jo Heathcote
Publisher: Katie Sergeant
Product developer: Roisin Leahy
Development editor: Jo Kemp
Copy editor: Gudrun Kaiser
Proofreader: Claire Throp
Cover designer: Amparo Barrera, Kneath Associates
Internal designer and typesetter: Hugh Hillyard-Parker
Production controller: Alhady Ali
Printed and bound in the UK using 100% Renewable Electricity at CPI Group (UK) Ltd

MIX
Paper from
responsible sources
FSC C007454

This book is produced from independently certified FSC™ paper to ensure responsible forest management.

For more information visit:
harpercollins.co.uk/green

Contents

Introduction	iv
Project overviews	v
Student progress trackers	viii
Year 7, *A Midsummer Night's Dream*	1
Year 8, *The Merchant of Venice*	48
Year 9, *Romeo and Juliet*	96
Acknowledgements	157

Introduction

Welcome to the *Reimagine Key Stage 3 Shakespeare* Teacher Resource.

I have always strongly believed in the teaching of whole Shakespeare plays at Key Stage 3. In my own classroom, I have always found – no matter the context or ability range of the students – that the teaching of Shakespeare, delivered with imagination and activity, can provide the most enriching and enjoyable way to develop students' knowledge and skills. Students who perhaps begin from a point of trepidation, never fail to be captivated by Shakespeare's characters, the twists and turns of the plots, and the vivid and evocative language. A study of Shakespeare opens up universal themes and, if handled well, allows us to consider human experience directly relevant to the diverse experiences of our students.

Following on from the success of *Reimagine Key Stage 3 English*, I wanted to use the same project-based approach to enable students at Key Stage 3 to experience whole Shakespeare plays in a way which is manageable and meaningful as part of their study.

Each year group is introduced to a key play:

- Year 7: *A Midsummer Night's Dream*
- Year 8: *The Merchant of Venice*
- Year 9: *Romeo and Juliet.*

The study of each play is organised into a six-week project. Each suggested 'week' comprises two lessons complete with extracts, PowerPoints, worksheets and detailed lesson plans with suggested responses to tasks and thoughtful prompts to develop meaningful classroom questioning. Each project follows a clear structure, working through the play as a whole, focusing on key scenes, with further reciprocal reading opportunities helpfully referenced to the *Collins Classroom Classics* editions of the plays.

Students have the opportunity to establish their understanding of plot and character through guided comprehension and inferential reading work, and to explore the beauty of Shakespeare's language through analysis and exploration. This study of the play is enhanced through opportunities to work on stagecraft to increase engagement with the text and to complete drama-focused activities to build confidence in speaking and listening.

As the lessons follow each play into into Act 4 and students have had the chance to conceptualise the themes of the play, the outcomes focus on creative writing opportunities as a response to the play's ideas, characters, language, imagery or plot.

Each project culminates in a reflective point of view activity which relates the play to a modern context and allows students to see the relevance of Shakespeare's themes.

I hope these projects create confident readers, and meaningful study of Shakespeare for students, enabling an enriching Key Stage 3 experience and providing valuable knowledge, skills and cultural capital to take forward into Key Stage 4.

Jo Heathcote
Author and Series Editor

Project overviews

Year 7: *A Midsummer Night's Dream*

Week	Skill focus	Text	Learning objectives
1.1	Comprehension and inference	Act 1 Scene 1 *'Full of vexation come I'*	To understand key ideas from the opening of the play. To develop first impressions of characters.
1.2	Understanding the theme of love Letter writing	Act 1 Scene 1 *'The course of true love never did run smooth'*	To explore Lysander's thoughts about love. To show knowledge and understanding of the plot through recasting.
2.1	Exploring character Describing a fairy character	Act 2 Scene 1, and Act 2 Scene 2 *'The King doth keep his revels here to-night'*	To understand ideas and images created by the fairy world.
2.2	Stagecraft: costume design	Act 2 Scene 1, and Act 2 Scene 2 *'Come, now a roundel and a fairy song'*	To explore the presentation of the fairies in the play. To design and label contrasting costumes for the fairy characters.
3.1	Language analysis and its effect/dramatic impact	Act 2 Scene 2 *'O, I am out of breath in this fond chase!'*	To understand how Shakespeare creates a plot twist for dramatic effect. To explore the techniques Shakespeare uses to create humour.
3.2	Language analysis connected to key characters	Act 2 Scene 2 *'What a dream was here!'*	To explore the changing language of the characters. To select and present the changing language of the characters in a language map.
4.1	Drama focus: exploring emotions	Act 3 Scene 1 *'I pray thee, gentle mortal, sing again.'*	To understand the way emotions are portrayed in a scene. To explore and present those ideas imaginatively.
4.2	Drama focus: developing understanding of character through hot seating	Act 3 Scene 2 *'Fie, fie! You counterfeit, you puppet you!'*	To understand the motivation and feelings of Hermia and Helena. To explore opinions through hot-seating.
5.1	Comprehension Language analysis: imagery	Act 4 Scene 1 *'The fierce vexation of a dream'*	To understand the development of the plot. To explore and create images of the natural world.
5.2	Descriptive writing	Act 4 Scene 1 *'It seems to me that yet we sleep, we dream.'*	To plan and write a description based on a picture. To use imagery to bring a description to life.
6.1	Exploring the themes of the play against a modern context	Act 2 Scene 1 *'The poet's eye... Doth glance from heaven to earth'*	To explore Shakespeare's possible message or intentions. To make contextual connections between the themes of the play and environmental issues today.
6.2	Persuasive writing: speeches	Act 2 Scene 1 *'And thorough this distemperature we see the seasons alter'*	To recap on basic persuasive techniques. To plan and write a short speech reflecting on the theme of the natural world.

Year 8: *The Merchant of Venice*

Week	Skill focus	Text	Learning objectives
1.1	Comprehension and inference	Act 1 Scene 1 'My purse, my person, my extremest means, Lie all unlock'd to your occasions'	To understand the characters of Bassanio and Antonio. To introduce Portia and her situation.
1.2	Critical reading connected to theme	Act 1 Scene 3 'For suff'rance is the badge of all our tribe'	To introduce Shylock and develop our understanding of key characters. To introduce the theme of prejudice.
2.1	Understanding and interpretation of plot	Act 2 Scene 7 'All that glisters is not gold'	To explore and interpret the messages on the caskets. To consider the implications of the casket test.
2.2	Stagecraft: prop design	Act 2 Scene 7 'Who chooseth me shall have as much as he deserves.'	To create a prop design for a casket symbolising the message it contains.
3.1	Language analysis Descriptive writing	Act 2 Scene 5 'Look to my house.'	To explore Shylock's use of language. To explore the image of the masque and create a contrasting description.
3.2	Language analysis and effect/dramatic impact	Act 2 Scene 3 'Love is blind'	To understand how Shakespeare presents Jessica. To consider how Shakespeare creates complex characters.
4.1	Drama focus: choral speech	Act 3 Scene 1 'If you prick us, do we not bleed?'	To understand how to present a viewpoint or perspective, using sound and movement. To explore opinions through choral speech.
4.2	Drama focus: improvisation	Act 3 Scene 3 '... since I am a dog, beware my fangs'	To explore the text through improvisation. To investigate writer intention and characterisation.
5.1	Close reading of a climactic scene	Act 4 Scene 1 'I crave the law'	To consolidate understanding of the trial scene. To consider the key themes of disguise and deception.
5.2	Narrative writing	Act 4 Scene 1 'I am arm'd and well prepar'd'	To understand the structure of a five-point narrative. To plan and write a narrative based on key ideas from the play.
6.1	Exploring a key speech Writing a soliloquy	Act 4 Scene 1 'The quality of mercy is not strain'd'	To explore key themes and ideas in the play. To reflect on the treatment of Shylock.
6.2	Presenting viewpoints: creating a podcast	Act 1, Scene 3 'Still have I borne it with a patient shrug'	To explore the wider issues and intentions of the play in a modern context.

Year 9: *Romeo and Juliet*

Week	Skill focus	Text	Learning objectives
1.1	Identify and retrieve Comprehension and inference	Act 1 Scene 1 'Rebellious subjects, enemies to peace'	To understand the conflict between the Montagues and Capulets. To introduce the character of Romeo.
1.2	Reading with fluency Group presentation of key ideas	Act 1 Scene 2, and Scene 3 'How stands your disposition to be married?'	To introduce the theme of love and marriage. To understand how Shakespeare presents different attitudes to love and marriage based on gender.
2.1	Exploration of language and structure Developed inferences related to character	Act 1 Scene 5 'She doth teach the torches to burn bright!'	To explore the initial meeting between Romeo and Juliet. To consider the images of fate, religion and concealment used to present their initial meeting.
2.2	Stagecraft: mask design	Act 1 Scene 5 'Too early seen unknown, and known too late!'	To create mask designs for Romeo and Juliet, symbolising their characters.
3.1	Close critical reading	Act 2 Scene 2 'If thou dost love, pronounce it faithfully'	To explore the development of Romeo and Juliet's relationship. To consider the risks they are taking and the consequences of their decision to marry.
3.2	Inferential reading Language analysis	Act 2 Scene 3, and Scene 5 'Wisely and slow; they stumble that run fast.'	To understand the thoughts and actions of the Friar and the Nurse. To explore how Shakespeare uses imagery to create the rising action.
4.1	Drama focus: freeze frame	Act 3 Scene 1 'And fire-ey'd fury be my conduct now!'	To understand how a scene is structured. To explore key moments through freeze frames.
4.2	Drama focus: forum theatre	Act 3 Scene 5 'I would the fool were married to her grave!'	To explore the wider themes and issues of the play. To debate ideas using Forum Theatre.
5.1	Language analysis Comprehension	Act 4 Scene 1 'past hope, past cure, past help'	To explore the language and imagery as Juliet faces a desperate situation. To understand the Friar's plan.
5.2	Narrative writing: recasting	Act 4 Scene 3 'Shall I be married, then, to-morrow morning?'	To reflect on the key ingredients of Shakespeare's plot. To recast the ingredients in a short story.
6.1	Comprehension Whole play recall	Act 5 Scene 1, and Scene 3 '…I defy you, stars.'	To understand the tragic conclusion to the play. To make connections from a key extract with the whole text.
6.2	Script writing	Act 5 Scene 3 'See what a scourge is laid upon your hate'	To work as a team to produce a script for a documentary exploring one of the key ideas from Shakespeare's play in a modern context.

Student progress trackers

Year 7: *A Midsummer Night's Dream*

Lesson focus	Key Skills Indicators *After completing these lessons I can:*	*How well do I understand this skill?* ☺ 😐 ☹	Comment and reflection
7.1.1 • Act 1 Sc 1 *'Full of vexation come I'* Date completed:	Make inferences about characters. Write a clear comprehension answer.		
7.1.2 • Act 1 Sc 1 *'The course of true love never did run smooth'* Date completed:	Show my understanding of the theme of love. Write a letter showing my knowledge of the plot.		
7.2.1 • Act 2 Sc 1 and 2 *'The King doth keep his revels here tonight'* Date completed:	Work in a team to explore a character from the magical world. Write a description of a fairy character.		
7.2.2 • Act 2 Sc 1 and 2 *'Come, now a roundel and a fairy song'* Date completed:	Think carefully about the presentation of a character in a production of the play. Create a design for contrasting fairy costumes.		
7.3.1 • Act 2 Sc 2 *'O, I am out of breath in this fond chase!'* Date completed:	Identify examples of language techniques. Write an analytical paragraph about language choices.		
7.3.2 • Act 2 Sc 2 *'What a dream was here!'* Date completed:	Select and retrieve examples of language. Create a language map showing the language of the four lovers.		

Year 7: *A Midsummer Night's Dream*

Lesson focus	Key Skills Indicators *After completing these lessons I can:*	*How well do I understand this skill?* ☺ 😐 ☹	Comment and reflection
7.4.1 • Act 3 Sc 1 *'I pray thee, gentle mortal, sing again.'* Date completed:	Work in a pair to present the emotions of the scene through sound and movement.		
7.4.2 • Act 3 Sc 2 *'Fie, fie! You counterfeit, you puppet you!'* Date completed:	Take part in a hot seating activity to understand more about characters.		
7.5.1 • Act 4 Sc 1 *'The fierce vexation of a dream'* Date completed:	Select examples of Shakespeare's imagery. Create my own imagery of a magical forest.		
7.5.2 • Act 4 Sc 1 *'It seems to me that yet we sleep, we dream.'* Date completed:	Plan and write a description of a magical forest.		
7.6.1 • Act 2 Sc 1 *'The poet's eye... Doth glance from heaven to earth'* Date completed:	Work in a group to explore Shakespeare's key messages.		
7.6.2 • Act 2 Sc 1 *'And thorough this distemperature we see the seasons alter'* Date completed:	Plan and write a short speech.		

Year 8: *The Merchant of Venice*

Lesson focus	Key Skills Indicators *After completing these lessons I can:*	*How well do I understand this skill?* ☺ 😐 ☹	Comment and reflection
8.1.1 • Act 1 Sc 1 **'My purse, my person, my extremest means, Lie all unlock'd to your occasions'** Date completed:	Make inferences about characters and present clear comprehension responses.		
8.1.2 • Act 1 Sc 3 **'For suff'rance is the badge of all our tribe'** Date completed:	Explore ideas connected to the theme of prejudice sensitively. Understand the key ideas connected to the plot.		
8.2.1 • Act 2 Sc 7 **'All that glisters is not gold'** Date completed:	Work in a group to explore the importance of the caskets. Develop my understanding of Portia.		
8.2.2 • Act 2 Sc 7 **'Who chooseth me shall have as much as he deserves.'** Date completed:	Produce an effective design for a key prop.		
8.3.1 • Act 2 Sc 5 **'Look to my house.'** Date completed:	Explore Shylock's language. Write a contrasting description.		
8.3.2 • Act 2 Sc 3 **'Love is blind'** Date completed:	Analyse the language used to present the character of Jessica.		

Year 8: *The Merchant of Venice*

Lesson focus	Key Skills Indicators *After completing these lessons I can:*	*How well do I understand this skill?* ☺ ☺ ☹	Comment and reflection
8.4.1 • Act 3 Sc 1 *'If you prick us, do we not bleed?'* Date completed:	Work in a group to perform Shylock's thoughts and opinions.		
8.4.2 • Act 3 Sc 3 *'... since I am a dog, beware my fangs'* Date completed:	Work in a pair to improvise an alternative scene.		
8.5.1 • Act 4 Sc 1 *'I crave the law'* Date completed:	Work in a group to explore a key scene. Work in a pair to explore the themes of disguise and deception.		
8.5.2 • Act 4 Sc 1 *'I am arm'd and well prepar'd'* Date completed:	Plan and write an effective narrative.		
8.6.1 • Act 4 Sc 1 *'The quality of mercy is not strain'd'* Date completed:	Work in pairs to explore Portia's speech. Create a soliloquy for Shylock.		
8.6.2 • Act 1 Sc 3 *'Still have I borne it with a patient shrug'* Date completed:	Work in a group to create a podcast reflecting on the key themes of the play.		

Year 9: *Romeo and Juliet*

Lesson focus	Key Skills Indicators *After completing these lessons I can:*	How well do I understand this skill? ☺ 😐 ☹	Comment and reflection
9.1.1 • Act 1 Sc 1 *'Rebellious subjects, enemies to peace'* Date completed:	Select and retrieve key information. Make inferences about character. Write a detailed comprehension response.		
9.1.2 • Act 1 Sc 2 and 3 *'How stands your disposition to be married?'* Date completed:	Work in a group to present a polished reading. Work in a group to present an exploration of the key ideas in a scene.		
9.2.1 • Act 1 Sc 5 *'She doth teach the torches to burn bright!'* Date completed:	Analyse the language and structure of Romeo and Juliet's first meeting. Understand Shakespeare's intentions.		
9.2.2 • Act 1 Sc 5 *'Too early seen unknown, and known too late!'* Date completed:	Create a mask symbolising a key character.		
9.3.1 • Act 2 Sc 2 *'If thou dost love, pronounce it faithfully'* Date completed:	Work in a pair to explore the development of the key characters. Make developed inferences.		
9.3.2 • Act 2 Sc 3 and 5 *'Wisely and slow; they stumble that run fast.'* Date completed:	Annotate an extract exploring thoughts and feelings of the Friar. Work independently to evaluate the actions of the Nurse.		

Year 9: *Romeo and Juliet*

Lesson focus	Key Skills Indicators *After completing these lessons I can:*	*How well do I understand this skill?* ☺ 😐 ☹	Comment and reflection
9.4.1 • Act 3 Sc 1 *'And fire-ey'd fury be my conduct now!'* Date completed:	To work in a group to produce freeze frames.		
9.4.2 • Act 3 Sc 5 *'I would the fool were married to her grave!'* Date completed:	Take part in a forum theatre exercise.		
9.5.1 • Act 4 Sc 1 *'past hope, past cure, past help'* Date completed:	Analyse the language, structure, and ideas of Juliet's speech. Understand the Friar's plan.		
9.5.2 • Act 4 Sc 3 *'Shall I be married, then, to-morrow morning?'* Date completed:	Plan and write a short story using the key ingredients from Romeo and Juliet.		
9.6.1 • Act 5 Sc 1 and 3 *'…I defy you, stars.'* Date completed:	Understand the conclusion of the play. Use Romeo's final speech to make links across the whole play.		
9.6.2 • Act 5 Sc 3 *'See what a scourge is laid upon your hate'* Date completed:	Work in a team to produce a script for a documentary.		

Extract 7.1.1
Act 1 Sc 1
'Full of vexation come I'

The story so far ...
The Duke of Athens, Theseus, is planning his wedding to the Queen of the Amazons, Hippolyta, whom he has defeated in a battle. A nobleman, Egeus, arrives and asks for the Duke's support. His daughter, Hermia, is refusing to marry Demetrius, the man he has chosen for her, because she is in love with another young Athenian, Lysander. However, her father demands that she should obey him and wants the Duke to help him with this.

Athens. The palace of Theseus

[Enter THESEUS, HIPPOLYTA, PHILOSTRATE and ATTENDANTS]

Theseus
Now, fair Hippolyta, our **nuptial hour**
Draws on apace; four happy days bring in
Another moon: but, O, methinks, how slow
This old moon wanes! She lingers my desires,
Like to a step-dame or a dowager, 5
Long withering out a young man's revenue.

Hippolyta
Four days will quickly steep themselves in night;
Four nights will quickly dream away the time;
And then the moon, like to a silver bow
New-bent in heaven, shall behold the night 10
Of our **solemnities**.

Theseus
Go, Philostrate,
Stir up the Athenian youth to merriments;
Awake the pert and nimble spirit of mirth;
Turn melancholy forth to funerals;
The pale companion is not for our pomp. 15

[Exit PHILOSTRATE]

Hippolyta, I woo'd thee with my sword,
And won thy love, doing thee injuries;
But I will wed thee in another key,
With pomp, with triumph, and with revelling.

[Enter EGEUS, and his daughter HERMIA, LYSANDER and DEMETRIUS]

Egeus
>Happy be Theseus, our renowned Duke! 20

Theseus
>Thanks, good Egeus; what's the news with thee?

Egeus
>Full of vexation come I, with complaint
>Against my child, my daughter Hermia.
>Stand forth, Demetrius. My noble lord,
>This man hath my consent to marry her. 25
>Stand forth, Lysander. And, my gracious Duke,
>This man hath bewitch'd the bosom of my child.
>Thou, thou, Lysander, thou hast given her rhymes,
>And interchang'd love-tokens with my child;
>Thou hast by moonlight at her window sung, 30
>With **feigning** voice verses of feigning love,
>And stol'n the impression of her fantasy
>With bracelets of thy hair, rings, **gawds, conceits,**
>**Knacks, trifles, nosegays, sweetmeats** – messengers
>Of strong prevailment in unhardened youth; 35
>With cunning hast thou **filch'd** my daughter's heart;
>Turn'd her obedience, which is due to me,
>To stubborn harshness. And, my gracious Duke,
>Be it so she will not here before your Grace
>Consent to marry with Demetrius, 40
>I beg the ancient privilege of Athens:
>As she is mine, I may dispose of her;
>Which shall be either to this gentleman
>Or to her death, according to our law
>Immediately provided in that case. 45

Glossary

nuptial hour: the time of our wedding

solemnities: wedding ceremony

feigning: false; deceitful

gawds, conceits, knacks, trifles, nosegays, sweetmeats: trinkets, little gifts, flowers, sweets

filch'd: stolen

Lesson 7.1.1 — *'Full of vexation come I'*

Learning objective(s):	Resources:
• To understand key ideas from the opening of the play. • To develop first impressions of characters.	• PowerPoint 7.1.1 • Extract 7.1.1 • Worksheet 7.1.1

Getting started

- Introduce the lesson objectives on **PowerPoint slide 1**. Then display **PowerPoint slide 2** and introduce students to the idea that the play they will be studying is set in Athens, Greece. Check prior knowledge: Do students know anything about Ancient Greece? Have they read any stories or myths connected with Ancient Greece? Use the images on the slide to prompt responses about battles, heroes, dress styles and buildings to set the scene for the opening of the play. Allocate parts and read **Extract 7.1.1** together as a whole class, using the glossary to explain unfamiliar vocabulary. Ensure that students know to read by sentence and not by line to make full sense of the text. Explain how punctuation marks such as dashes and semicolons create a longer pause than a comma to assist the fluency of their reading. You could model this by taking one of the parts yourself or reading the opening speech to demonstrate.

Developing skills

- Show **PowerPoint slide 3** and ask students to work in pairs to explore the questions. Take feedback to check their understanding. Students should have picked up on: *Theseus is looking forward to his wedding day; Hippolyta reassures him by saying the time will pass quickly; Egeus is angry with his daughter and with Lysander, who he believes has bewitched her; he asks the Duke to ensure that Hermia obeys him or is put to death.*

- Hand out **Worksheet 7.1.1** and direct students to **Activity 1**. For a), allow time for students to select some of the lines from the extract and list them in their own words, then add the lines from the extract. Using the evidence they have collected, ask students to write a sentence or two for b), concluding by stating whether they think the things Lysander has done can be considered 'bewitching'. Share some responses with the class.

- Display **PowerPoint Slide 4** and, with the whole class, develop deeper thinking by focusing on the character of Egeus. Ask students for their thoughts and ideas about how they view this character. What kind of a father do they feel he is? Might this be usual at the time for wealthy families? How do students respond to the idea that Hermia is spoken of as a possession? How do they feel about the harsh choice she is given? What about the fact that Egeus takes her to the Duke? Conclude with some discussion about Hermia's feelings in all this. How do students respond? Can they imagine being Hermia or Lysander at this point?

- Now use **PowerPoint slide 5** to model how students might present clear comprehension answers to consolidate their thoughts on plot and character. Make sure students are aware that all good comprehension responses begin with a clear statement that addresses the focus of the question. Explain that the quotation should not paraphrase either the statement or the inference but should support the statement. Point out the conventions of punctuation in the supporting quotation, for example, the use of quotation marks, the direct quotation of the text within them, the use of the comma prior to the quotation, the full stop before the new sentence of the inference. Explain how an inference is the measure of our understanding and comes from us as readers, not from the text. Use the comparison of 'reading between the lines of a text' with students and explain how the inference is something that is not said in the text, but something we might deduce, like a 'reading detective'. Inferences might begin in several ways to trigger that thought and these are exemplified on the slide.

Trying it yourself

- Ask students to do **Activity 2** on the worksheet, to try the comprehension method for themselves, following the model on **PowerPoint slide 5**. Take some feedback from students about the different statements they have made, quotations they have chosen and inferences they have drawn from their study so far.

Worksheet 7.1.1 — 'Full of vexation come I'

In the text, Egeus accuses Lysander of 'bewitching' his daughter.

Activity 1

a) Using your own words, make a list in the table of some of the things Egeus feels Lysander has done to 'bewitch' Hermia. Then add the lines from the extract that tell you this.

Egeus feels that Lysander has …	Lines from the extract

b) Do you believe Hermia has been bewitched by Lysander? Write your thoughts here in a clear sentence.

....

....

Activity 2

Answer the following comprehension question, using the model on the slide to help you.

What do we understand about the character of Egeus from the text so far?

Statement: ....

....

Quotation: ....

....

Inference: ....

....

Extract 7.1.2 Act 1 Sc 1
'The course of true love never did run smooth'

The story continues ...

Following Egeus's complaints, Hermia bravely says that she will not marry Demetrius but that she truly loves Lysander. The Duke decrees that Hermia has three choices: to marry Demetrius, to enter a convent and live the life of a nun, or to face death. Left alone, the lovers Hermia and Lysander reflect on their situation.

Lysander
How now, my love! Why is your cheek so pale?
How chance the roses there do fade so fast?

Hermia
Belike for want of rain, which I could well   130
Beteem them from the tempest of my eyes.

Lysander
Ay me! for aught that I could ever read,
Could ever hear by tale or history,
The course of true love never did run smooth;
But, either it was different in blood—   135

Hermia
O cross! too high to be enthrall'd to low.

Lysander
Or else **misgraffed** in respect of years—

Hermia
O spite! too old to be engaged to young.

Lysander
Or else it stood upon the choice of friends—

Hermia
O hell! to choose love by another's eyes.   140

Lysander
Or, if there were a sympathy in choice,
War, death, or sickness, did lay siege to it,
Making it momentary as a sound,
Swift as a shadow, short as any dream,
Brief as the lightning in the **collied** night   145
That, **in a spleen**, unfolds both heaven and earth,

And ere a man hath power to say 'Behold!'
The jaws of darkness do devour it up;
So quick bright things come to confusion.

Hermia

If then true lovers have been ever cross'd,   150
It stands as an **edict** in destiny.
Then let us teach our trial patience,
Because it is a customary cross,
As due to love as thoughts and dreams and sighs,
Wishes and tears, poor Fancy's followers.   155

Lysander

A good persuasion; therefore, hear me, Hermia.
I have a widow aunt, a dowager
Of great **revenue**, and she hath no child—
From Athens is her house remote seven **leagues**—
And she respects me as her only son.   160
There, gentle Hermia, may I marry thee;
And to that place the sharp Athenian law
Cannot pursue us. If thou lovest me then,
Steal forth thy father's house to-morrow night;
And in the wood, a league without the town,   165
Where I did meet thee once with Helena
To do observance to a morn of May,
There will I stay for thee.

Glossary

misgraffed: mismatched

collied: blackened

in a spleen: in a flash of temper

edict: law

revenue: wealth

league: one league is about three miles

Lesson 7.1.2 — 'The course of true love never did run smooth'

Learning objective(s):	Resources:
• To explore Lysander's thoughts about love. • To show knowledge and understanding of the plot through recasting.	• PowerPoint 7.1.2 • Extract 7.1.2 • Worksheet 7.1.2

Recap and reflection

- Show **PowerPoint slide 1** and share the lesson objectives with the class. Reflect on prior learning using the prompt questions on **PowerPoint slide 2**. Take responses from the class so that students can mark themselves: *Egeus was angry with Hermia for defying his wishes; he wanted the Duke to support his wishes that she marry Demetrius or face death; Hermia loves Lysander; her father wants her to marry Demetrius.*

- With the class, read **The story continues ...** and the glossary words for **Extract 7.1.2** to consolidate knowledge. Then allocate the parts or ask students to read the extract in pairs.

Developing skills

- Display **PowerPoint slide 3** and ask students to work in pairs to explore the first two questions and then make a list of Lysander's reasons and observations about love. Check these together in a whole-group plenary. Answers might include that the lovers: *are from different races, cultures or backgrounds; they have an age difference; their friends might not approve of their choice or like them; conflict or illness or even death might separate them suddenly.*

Trying it yourself

- Once students' knowledge is secure, hand out **Worksheet 7.1.2** and ask them to work individually to visualise these reasons, creating sketches to illustrate each one. Encourage students to be imaginative and perhaps introduce the idea of personifying love, or using a symbol such as a heart to represent love.

Final task

- The final task allows students to consolidate their knowledge from both lessons so far and show their knowledge and understanding of the plot. Display **PowerPoint slide 4** and explain that, writing in character as Lysander, students are going to compose a letter to the aunt that includes the key information listed on the slide.

- Use **PowerPoint slide 5** to model some of the key elements of letter layout and the success criteria for the task. Ask students to work individually or in pairs to write the letter in their own notebooks, ready for assessment.

Taking it further

- Follow up with a reciprocal reading lesson by completing a read of Act 1, from pages 15 to 29 of *Collins Classroom Classics*, introducing the character of Helena at the end of Scene 1 and the Mechanicals (the play's clowns/workmen: Quince, Snug, Bottom, Flute, Snout and Starveling) in Scene 2. Alternatively, students could watch a performance or film version of Act 1, such as those available to stream online from Shakespeare's Globe Theatre, the National Theatre or the RSC.

Worksheet 7.1.2: 'The course of true love never did run smooth'

Activity

Create a comic-book style sketch in each of the boxes below to illustrate the reasons that true love does not go to plan, according to Lysander.

'Either it was different in blood'	'Or else misgraffed in respect of years'
'Or else it stood upon the choice of friends'	**'War, death, or sickness, did lay siege to it'**
'Making it momentary as a ... shadow, short as any dream'	**'The jaws of darkness do devour it up'**

Extract 7.2.1
Act 2 Sc 1
Act 2 Sc 2

'The King doth keep his revels here to-night'

The story continues …

The setting changes to the forest, which is a magical world inhabited by fairies. We meet Puck, the mischievous fairy who serves the Fairy King Oberon. We learn that there is a conflict between Oberon and the Fairy Queen, Titania, which is unsettling the natural world. Oberon wants Titania to give him a changeling boy to be his page. She refuses as she has vowed to care for him. Oberon decides to put a spell on her for revenge.

A wood near Athens

[Enter a FAIRY at one door, and PUCK at another]

Puck

How now, spirit! whither wander you?

Fairy

Over hill, over dale,
Thorough bush, thorough brier,
Over park, over pale,
Thorough flood, thorough fire, 5
I do wander every where,
Swifter than the moon's sphere;
And I serve the Fairy Queen,
To dew her orbs upon the green.
The cowslips tall her pensioners be; 10
In their gold coats spots you see;
Those be rubies, fairy favours,
In those freckles live their savours.

I must go seek some dewdrops here,
And hang a pearl in every cowslip's ear. 15
Farewell, thou lob of spirits; I'll be gone.
Our Queen and all her elves come here anon.

Puck

The King doth keep his revels here to-night;
Take heed the Queen come not within his sight;
For Oberon is passing fell and wrath, 20
Because that she as her attendant hath
A lovely boy, stolen from an Indian king.
She never had so sweet a **changeling**;

And jealous Oberon would have the child
Knight of his train, to trace the forests wild;   25
But she perforce withholds the loved boy,
Crowns him with flowers, and makes him all her joy.
And now they never meet in grove or green,
By fountain clear, or spangled starlight sheen,
But they do **square**, that all their elves for fear   30
Creep into acorn cups and hide them there.

[...]

Another part of the wood

[Enter TITANIA, *with her train]*

Titania

Come now, a roundel and a fairy song;
Then, for the third part of a minute, hence:
Some to kill **cankers** in the musk-rose buds,
Some war with **rere-mice** for their leathern wings,
To make my small elves coats, and some keep back   5
The clamorous owl that nightly hoots and wonders
At our quaint spirits. Sing me now asleep;
Then to your offices and let me rest.

[The FAIRIES *sing]*

1st Fairy

You spotted snakes with double tongue,
Thorny hedgehogs, be not seen;   10
Newts and blind-worms, do no wrong,
Come not near our fairy Queen.

Chorus

Philomel, with melody
Sing in our sweet lullaby.
Lulla, lulla, lullaby; lulla, lulla, lullaby.   15
Never harm
Nor spell nor charm
Come our lovely lady nigh.
So good night, with lullaby.

2nd Fairy

Weaving spiders, come not here;   20
Hence, you long-legg'd spinners, hence.
Beetles black, approach not near;
Worm nor snail do no offence.

Chorus

        Philomel with melody, etc.

        [TITANIA sleeps]

1st Fairy

    Hence away; now all is well.   25
    One aloof stand sentinel.

    [Exeunt FAIRIES Enter OBERON and squeezes the flower on TITANIA's eyelids]

Oberon

    What thou seest when thou dost wake,
    Do it for thy true-love take;
    Love and languish for his sake.
    Be it ounce, or cat, or bear,   30
    Pard, or boar with bristled hair,
    In thy eye that shall appear
    When thou wak'st, it is thy dear.
    Wake when some vile thing is near.

Glossary

changeling: a human child taken by fairies

square: argue

cankers: disease

rere-mice: bats

Lesson 7.2.1 — *'The King doth keep his revels here to-night'*

Learning objective(s):	Resources:
• To understand ideas and images created by the fairy world.	• PowerPoint 7.2.1 • Extract 7.2.1

Getting started

- Share the lesson objective on **PowerPoint slide 1** with the class. Use the prompts on **PowerPoint slide 2** with the whole class to introduce ideas connected to fairies. Students may be able to suggest things such as: *the idea that fairies are small, magical creatures; they can fly; they can be found in films and stories such as Tinkerbell, and in our imagination, for example the Tooth Fairy; associated with woodland or toadstools.*

- Develop students' thinking for the final prompt by showing the images on **PowerPoint slide 3**, which show fireflies in a woodland and a damselfly. How might natural creatures such as these have made older/more ancient peoples and cultures create myths around fairies?

- Use **The story continues** … to introduce **Extract 7.2.1**. The extracts are drawn from both scenes in Act 2. Allocate parts and ask students to read the extracts aloud.

Developing skills

- Now divide the class into small groups, with half of the groups working as Team Puck and half working as Team Titania. Set team tasks from **PowerPoint slides 4** and **5**. Allow students time to work in their teams to re-read the extracts and then explore the prompt questions, noting down their ideas or making use of a scribe. Allow time for teams to feed back their thoughts and ideas.

- Encourage Team Puck to identify: *that rhyming couplets are used; that fairies can move in a supernatural and speedy way; that Oberon is cross with the Fairy Queen and wants to have her 'changeling boy'; that this conflict is causing fear among the fairy kingdom – even the elves are hiding.*

- Encourage Team Titania to identify: *that the fairies are instructed to cure the diseases in the roses, attack bats to take their wings, and keep the owl out of the way; that the object of the lullaby is to weave a spell of protection around her; however, Oberon places the spell, which is designed to make her fall in love with a 'vile creature' when she wakes.* You could take this opportunity to introduce the idea of dramatic irony here in that we as the audience know what is going to happen to Titania, whereas she is unaware of Oberon's actions.

Trying it yourself

- Display **PowerPoint slide 6**. Ask students to work individually in their notebooks to consolidate their knowledge of the fairies by reflecting on what they have learned and understood about Puck, Titania and Oberon at this point. Students should create mind maps for each of the three main fairy characters. If time allows, you could scaffold this task by showing a clip from a streamed production of these two scenes up to the point where Titania is sleeping.

- Students should then select one character to focus on and move on to the final task on the slide in which students write a description of their chosen character, including their collection of words, phrases and quotations from their mind map. Encourage students to be as imaginative as possible but to base their description on the ideas they have shared and gathered from the text.

- You may wish to ask students to prepare for the next lesson by bringing in a selection of their own art and craft materials, or prepare a selection of your own.

Lesson 7.2.2 — *'Come now, a roundel and a fairy song'*

Learning objective(s):	Resources:
• To explore the presentation of the fairies in the play. • To design and label contrasting costumes for the fairy characters.	• PowerPoint 7.2.2 • Extract 7.2.1 • Worksheet 7.2.2 • Plain A4 paper and craft materials for worksheet activity

It is useful to prepare art and craft materials for the worksheet before the lesson, or ask students in advance to bring materials to the lesson.

Recap and reflection

- Share the lesson objectives on **PowerPoint slide 1** with the class. Use **PowerPoint slide 2** to reflect on key ideas from the previous lesson. Encourage students to recall how Titania and Oberon were in conflict and that this has had repercussions in the natural world. Recap Oberon's spell and what his unkind intentions are for Titania.

Developing skills

- Display **PowerPoint slide 3** and explore the idea of the challenge for costume designers with the whole class. How might they make actors look like they are part of the magical world? How might they give the impression that they are small, magical creatures? How might a designer create the idea of the different temperaments and power of the fairies, especially the King and Queen? Use the images on the slide, if appropriate to your setting, to show possibilities, or visit online image galleries of past productions such as those at the RSC, Globe Theatre and National Theatre.

Final task

- Distribute sheets of plain A4 paper and allow students the remainder of the lesson time (and possibly homework time too) to create their two contrasting designs as outlined on **Worksheet 7.2.2**.

Taking it further

- Follow up with a reciprocal reading lesson, completing a read of Act 2 scenes 1 and part of 2, pages 33 to 53 of *Collins Classroom Classics*, developing the detail of Oberon's anger with Titania and expanding on why she won't give up the boy. We also see Helena following Demetrius into the woods in this scene and his rejection of her advances. Alternatively, students could watch a performance or film version of this scene, such as the ones available to stream online from Shakespeare's Globe Theatre, the National Theatre or the RSC.

Worksheet 7.2.2: 'Come now, a roundel and a fairy song'

Activity

Imagine that your school is going to do a production of *A Midsummer Night's Dream*. You have been asked to produce costume designs to show two different sides of the fairy world. Design a costume that shows the fairies as:

a) spiteful, quick-tempered and angry creatures who cause chaos in the natural world

b) creatures who belong and are at peace in the natural environment of the forest.

Produce your designs on plain paper and keep them neat.

Include information about and sketches of:

- the fabric, colours and textures you would use (use art and craft materials and paste them on your drawing to give a more realistic effect)
- the style of the costume (don't forget wings or cloaks!)
- any accessories such as jewellery, headdresses, make-up of props (perhaps made of twigs, leaves or berries).

Add your collected descriptive words, phrases and quotations from your mind maps around your designs to add to the effect.

Begin by writing some planning notes below:

Extract 7.3.1
Act 2 Sc 2

'O, I am out of breath in this fond chase!'

The story continues ...

Lysander and Hermia meet in the forest that night to begin their escape from Athens. Before leaving, they confide in Helena, Hermia's friend since childhood, that they are going. Helena is deeply in love with Demetrius and the eloping couple feel they will be helping her by telling her of their escape. Desperate to win his favour, Helena tells Demetrius of the secret plan. He is enraged that Lysander is eloping with Hermia and rushes into the forest, pursued by Helena. Oberon sees that Helena is upset that Demetrius rejects her and asks Puck to use the same flower juice love potion that he used on Titania to make Demetrius love Helena. Lysander and Hermia, meanwhile, become lost in the forest and settle down to sleep until it's light.

[Enter DEMETRIUS and HELENA, running]

Helena
　　Stay, though thou kill me, sweet Demetrius.

Demetrius
　　I **charge** thee, hence, and do not haunt me thus.　　85

Helena
　　O, wilt thou **darkling leave me**? Do not so.

Demetrius
　　Stay, on thy peril: I alone will go.

[Exit DEMETRIUS]

Helena
　　O, I am out of breath in this fond chase!
　　The more my prayer, the lesser is my grace.
　　Happy is Hermia, wheresoe'er she lies,　　90
　　For she hath blessed and attractive eyes.
　　How came her eyes so bright? Not with salt tears;
　　If so, my eyes are oft'ner wash'd than hers.
　　No, no, I am as ugly as a bear,
　　For beasts that meet me run away for fear;　　95
　　Therefore no marvel though Demetrius
　　Do, as a monster, fly my presence thus.
　　What wicked and **dissembling glass** of mine
　　Made me compare with Hermia's **sphery eyne**?
　　But who is here? Lysander! on the ground!　　100

>   Dead, or asleep? I see no blood, no wound.
>   Lysander, if you live, good sir, awake.
>
> *Lysander [Waking]*
>   And run through fire I will for thy sweet sake.
>   Transparent Helena! Nature shows art,
>   That through thy bosom makes me see thy heart.   105
>   Where is Demetrius? O, how fit a word
>   Is that vile name to perish on my sword!
>
> *Helena*
>   Do not say so, Lysander; say not so.
>   What though he love your Hermia? Lord, what though?
>   Yet Hermia still loves you; then be content.   110
>
> *Lysander*
>   Content with Hermia! No: I do repent
>   The tedious minutes I with her have spent.
>   Not Hermia but Helena I love:
>   Who will not change a raven for a dove?
>   The will of man is by his reason sway'd,   115
>   And reason says you are the worthier maid.
>   Things growing are not ripe until their season;
>   So I, being young, till now ripe not to reason;
>   And touching now the point of human skill,
>   Reason becomes the marshal to my will,   120
>   And leads me to your eyes, where I o'erlook
>   Love's stories, written in Love's richest book.
>
> *Helena*
>   Wherefore was I to this keen mockery born?
>   When at your hands did I deserve this scorn?
>   Is't not enough, is't not enough, young man,   125
>   That I did never, no, nor never can,
>   Deserve a sweet look from Demetrius' eye,
>   But you must **flout my insufficiency**?
>   Good troth, you do me wrong, good sooth, you do,
>   In such disdainful manner me to woo.   130
>   But fare you well; perforce I must confess
>   I thought you lord of more true gentleness.
>   O, that a lady of one man refused
>   Should of another therefore be abus'd!

Glossary

charge: command

darkling leave me: leave me feeling sad and disappointed

dissembling glass: a mirror that seems to lie to her

sphery eyne: eyes like the stars

flout my insufficiency: mock my unattractiveness

Lesson 7.3.1 — 'O, I am out of breath in this fond chase!'

Learning objective(s):	**Resources:**
• To understand how Shakespeare creates a plot twist for dramatic effect. • To explore the techniques Shakespeare uses to create humour.	• PowerPoint 7.3.1 • Extract 7.3.1 • Worksheet 7.3.1

Getting started

- Show **PowerPoint slide 1** and share the lesson objectives with the class. Using **Extract 7.3.1**, read aloud **The story continues …** before displaying **PowerPoint slide 2**. Students should recall why Oberon put a spell on Titania – take suggestions from students about how they feel about his actions. What kind of a character do they think Oberon is to be doing this? Vengeful? Aggressive? Mean? Now ask students to consider the fact that Oberon sees that Helena is in distress and instructs Puck to help her. What side of Oberon does this show? Is everything as it seems in the forest and in the realm of the fairies? How does this link to their contrasting costume designs? How does this link to the world of nature?

Developing skills

- Display **PowerPoint slide 3** and introduce the idea of the plot twist to the class. Read aloud Puck's speech on the slide or invite a confident reader in the class to do this. Consolidate that Puck has placed the spell on the wrong man. Take some predictions and suggestions as to what might happen. Who else is in the forest that night? What might be the possible consequences?

- Ask students to work in groups of three to read **Extract 7.3.1** collaboratively. Remaining in their groups, ask students to complete the activity on **PowerPoint slide 4**. Allow students time to explore and consider the language choices here before sharing their thoughts. Suggested responses might include: *blessed, attractive, bright; I am as ugly as a bear; she views herself as unattractive – so much so that even creatures in the forest run away from her.* Encourage students to think more deeply through developed questioning: How is Helena feeling here? Why do they think she focuses on her appearance? How does she feel in comparison with Hermia? What feelings do students think she is experiencing? Are they positive or negative, for example, jealousy, despair?

- Distribute **Worksheet 7.3.1** and ask students, working in the same small groups, to complete **Activity 1**, highlighting key lines of the dialogue that link to the emotions in the list and then labelling them with the correct emotion. For example, Helena's opening line could be labelled *Despair*; Lysander's line *'Not Hermia but Helena I love'* could be labelled *Passion*. Allow some time for students to share suggested responses with the rest of the class.

- Add to students' knowledge by going through the definitions on **PowerPoint slide 5** before asking them to work on **Activity 2** on the worksheet. This could be done individually or in pairs for support. Encourage students to see the connection between the feeling or emotion created and the technique that Shakespeare uses.

Trying it yourself

- Using **PowerPoint slide 6**, model how students can present analytical paragraphs that explore techniques. Encourage students to note that they should first identify the technique and give it its correct term, then give a precise example. Finally, they should make a comment on the effect or impact of that technique on them as readers/the audience.

- Ask students to work individually, following the model, to write up at least one idea from **Activity 2** in this analytical format.

- If time allows, students could reconvene in the small groups they were working in earlier in the lesson and re-read or volunteer to perform the extract again, this time considering what they have discovered about the different feelings and emotions they should attach to each line and the development of the dialogue to create humour.

Worksheet 7.3.1 — 'O, I am out of breath in this fond chase!'

In this part of the play, Shakespeare uses several different techniques to begin to create humour in the play. The humour is created as we see the different reactions and changing moods of the characters to the situation they are in.

Activity 1

Using your copy of the extract, highlight a line of dialogue that shows one of the characters feeling the following emotions. Label each of your highlighted lines with the emotion you have chosen. You may use each word more than once if you wish.

- Confusion
- Anger
- Passion
- Outrage
- Despair
- Desperation
- Jealousy
- Scorn
- Offence

Activity 2

Now let's think about the ways Shakespeare creates all those different and changing emotions in such a short space of time. Complete the table below with at least one example of each technique we can find in the exchange between Demetrius and Helena and then Lysander. An example has been given to help you get started.

Shakespeare's technique	Used by which character?	Example from the extract	What feeling or emotion does this create?
Use of simile			
Use of imperatives or commands			
Use of questions	Helena	'Wherefore was I to this keen mockery born?'	Helena is offended by Lysander's declaration of love.
Use of exclamations			
Use of contrast or comparison			

Extract 7.3.2
Act 2 Sc 2
'What a dream was here!'

The story continues ...
Lysander, under the influence of the flower juice potion, pursues a confused and offended Helena into the forest, leaving Hermia alone and still asleep.

Lysander
> She sees not Hermia. Hermia, sleep thou there;   135
> And never mayst thou come Lysander near!
> For as a surfeit of the sweetest things
> The deepest loathing to the stomach brings,
> Or as the heresies that men do leave
> Are hated most of those they did deceive,   140
> So thou, my surfeit and my heresy,
> Of all be hated, but the most of me!
> And, all my powers, address your love and might
> To honour Helen, and to be her knight!

[Exit]

Hermia [Starting]
> Help me, Lysander, help me; do thy best   145
> To pluck this crawling serpent from my breast.
> Ay me, for pity! What a dream was here!
> Lysander, look how I do quake with fear.
> Methought a serpent eat my heart away,
> And you sat smiling at his cruel prey.   150
> Lysander! What, **remov'd**? Lysander! lord!
> What, out of hearing gone? No sound, no word?
> Alack, where are you? Speak, and if you hear;
> Speak, of all loves! I **swoon** almost with fear.
> No? then I well perceive you are not nigh.   155
> Either death or you I'll find immediately.

[Exit]

Glossary
remov'd: gone away
swoon: faint

Lesson 7.3.2   *'What a dream was here!'*

Learning objective(s):	Resources:
• To explore the changing language of the characters. • To select and present the changing language of the characters in a language map.	• PowerPoint 7.3.2 • Extracts 7.3.1 and 7.3.2 • Worksheet 7.3.2 • A4 or A3 paper

Recap and reflection

- Show **PowerPoint slide 1** and share the lesson objectives with the class. Ask students to reflect on the key aspects of the plot so far by completing the blank spaces in the sentences on **PowerPoint slide 2**. This could be done individually or collaboratively on the slide for more support. Answers are: *1. Asleep; make her fall in love with whatever she sees when she wakes. 2. Demetrius; Helena 3. Lysander; Helena 4. Helena; Lysander 5. Hermia.*

- Show **PowerPoint slide 3** if appropriate for your setting and use this to work with the whole class to reflect on Lysander and Hermia's relationship at the start of the play. How did they feel about each other? What risk did Hermia take for them to be together? What risks were they taking in leaving Athens? Ask students to work in pairs to note down as many words and phrases as they can to describe the couple and their love, for example: devoted, innocent, trusting, loving.

Developing skills

- Now work with the whole class to look at Lysander's language on **PowerPoint slide 4**. Explain to students that this is the speech he makes once Helena has left him. You may need to explain vocabulary such as 'surfeit' (too much) and 'heresy' (a false belief). Ask students to comment on how Lysander behaves here; what change do they notice in his language and feelings? How would they describe his language and his mood here? How surprising is it? What impact has the magic spell had on Lysander's feelings? How have Oberon's good intentions backfired?

- Distribute **Worksheet 7.3.2** and **Extract 7.3.2**. Use **The story continues …** on **Extract 7.3.2** to lead into Hermia's speech. Read this speech aloud. Ask students to work in pairs on **Activity 1**, adding their responses to their notebooks. Take some time to allow students to feed back on some of their responses. Push students to consider the idea of the serpent and why this might be part of Hermia's dream. In what ways has the forest and the natural world become her 'enemy'? Draw attention to her image of Lysander *'smiling at his cruel prey'*. How does this reflect the language Lysander was using about her previously?

- Still in their pairs, allow some time for students to work on **Activity 2**, selecting and retrieving examples of the language each character uses either in relation to or about another. Students should also reflect and consider adjectives to describe that language in each case. Some examples have been added to aid understanding. Students should use **Extract 7.3.1** and **Extract 7.3.2** for this exercise.

Final task

- Give each student a sheet of A4 or A3 plain paper. Display **PowerPoint Slide 5** and read through the task with students. Encourage them to begin with a forest outline using the image on the slide. They could add trees, bushes, boulders, streams and so on. Managing timing carefully, ask students to add the figures of the four lovers in different places on their map, allowing space around them to add words and phrases. Around each character students should write words and phrases that the characters use in relation to and about the other characters, in line with the bullet points on the slide. Students will be able to draw on their work from **Worksheet 7.3.2 Activity 2** to help them here.

- In plenary, ask students to reflect on the changing language of the lovers. How have all their feelings and attitudes changed? Has the magic had a positive or a negative impact on their relationships? Is Shakespeare presenting us with a moral here about love and relationships?

Taking it further

- Follow up with a reciprocal reading lesson of Act 3 scene 1 pages 63 to 73 of *Collins Classroom Classics*, until Titania awakens. Or, watch a version of all of Act 2 Scene 2 and the start of Act 3, such as those available to stream online from Shakespeare's Globe Theatre, the National Theatre or the RSC.

Worksheet 7.3.2 — 'What a dream was here!'

Activity 1

Working in pairs, look closely at Hermia's speech when she awakes and finds herself alone in the forest.

- How many exclamations are in this speech?
- How many questions are in this speech?
- How many imperatives are in this speech?
- What different feelings or emotions do you think Hermia is experiencing at this point?
- What words or phrases in her speech suggest that she has had a nightmare?
- What does her nightmare make you imagine? What do you think it might mean?

Activity 2

Look back through **Extract 7.3.1** and **Extract 7.3.2** and think about the language that the characters use about each other. Find examples and add them to the table below. Some examples have been given to help get you started.

What words and phrases does ...	Selected words and phrases	How would you describe their language? e.g. rude, loving, surprising
Demetrius use to Helena	'do not haunt me thus'	Aggressive, angry
Helena use to describe Hermia		
Lysander use when he wakes and sees Helena		
Lysander use about Hermia once he is under the spell	'deepest loathing to the stomach'	Hateful, cruel, surprising
Hermia use to Lysander when she wakes		

Extract 7.4.1
Act 3 Sc 1
'I pray thee, gentle mortal, sing again.'

The story continues ...

All four of the lovers, Demetrius, Lysander, Hermia and Helena, are wandering separately in the forest. However, Lysander is now under the influence of the magic flower juice. Titania is under the influence of the same magic and is also sleeping in the forest with her fairy train.

In the early morning come a band of workmen from Athens: the Mechanicals. They are here to rehearse a play to entertain Theseus and Hippolyta on their wedding day. Keen to cause mischief, Puck casts a spell to place a donkey's head on Nick Bottom, the weaver, which frightens away his companions and leaves him to wander, confused, in the forest ...

Titania
    What angel wakes me from my flow'ry bed?

Bottom [Sings]
    The finch, the sparrow, and the lark,   120
    The plain-song cuckoo grey,
    Whose note full many a man doth mark,
    And dares not answer nay—

    for, indeed, who would set his wit to so foolish a bird?
    Who would give a bird the lie, though he cry 'cuckoo'   125
    never so?

Titania
    I pray thee, gentle mortal, sing again.
    Mine ear is much **enamoured of** thy note;
    So is mine eye **enthralled to** thy shape;
    And thy fair virtue's force perforce doth move me,   130
    On the first view, to say, to swear, I love thee.

Bottom
    Methinks, mistress, you should have little reason for
    that. And yet, to say the truth, reason and love keep
    little company together now-a-days. The more the pity
    that some honest neighbours will not make them   135
    friends. Nay, I can **gleek** upon occasion.

Titania
    Thou art as wise as thou art beautiful.

Bottom
>Not so, neither; but if I had wit enough to get out of
>this wood, I have enough to serve mine own turn.

Titania
>Out of this wood do not desire to go; 140
>Thou shalt remain here whether thou wilt or no.
>I am a spirit of no **common rate**;
>The summer still doth tend upon my state;
>And I do love thee; therefore, go with me.
>I'll give thee fairies to attend on thee; 145
>And they shall fetch thee jewels from **the deep**,
>And sing, while thou on pressed flowers dost sleep;
>And I will purge thy mortal grossness so
>That thou shalt like an airy spirit go.
>Peaseblossom! Cobweb! Moth! and Mustardseed! 150

Glossary

enamoured of: delighted by

enthralled to: held spellbound by

gleek: make a clever joke

common rate: ordinary rank

the deep: the sea

Lesson 7.4.1 — *'I pray thee, gentle mortal, sing again.'*

Learning objective(s):
- To understand the way emotions are portrayed in a scene.
- To explore and present those ideas imaginatively.

Resources:
- PowerPoint 7.4.1
- Extract 7.4.1
- Worksheet 7.4.1

Getting started

- Display **PowerPoint slide 1** and share the lesson objectives with the class. Ask students for the names of some emotions. Encourage answers that are less obvious, such as shame, ecstasy, bashfulness.

- Get started by reading **Extract 7.4.1**. Use **The story continues ...** and the glossary to consolidate students' knowledge. Then allocate the parts or ask students to read in pairs.

- Use the prompt questions on **PowerPoint slide 2**. Take responses from the class to develop students' understanding: *1. Titania's emotions are heightened and could be described as, for example, joyous, ecstatic, loving; 2. Bottom reacts in a matter-of-fact way, as he just wants to find a way out of the woods; 3. Shakespeare makes the scene funny by contrasting the beautiful Titania with the unsightly Bottom with a donkey's head – the way the characters speak and react feed in to the humorous tone.*

Developing skills

- Display **PowerPoint slide 3**. Ask students to work in pairs to explore the scene through sound and gesture. They should first discuss and try out sounds that express the emotions in the scene. Encourage any sensible suggestions. For example, Bottom could whistle as he enters to show his carefree attitude; Titania could sigh as she wakes and sees him. Note that it is not necessary for students to speak the lines.

- Stop and check that each pair has some emotions to enact through sound.

- Now ask pairs to think of movements or gestures to accompany the sounds. Tell them to practise the scene using both sound and gesture to communicate emotion but without dialogue. For example, when Titania tells Bottom she loves him, she could stare intently with her hand on her heart. Bottom could react by staring at the ground in a shy manner.

- Give pairs time to develop their ideas. They should rehearse the emotions each character feels. Note that the scenes will not take as long to perform as they would if dialogue was being used.

Trying it yourself

- In your performance space, get ready to watch each pair's work. Decide whether to see all of them or just a few. Remind students that when we watch other people perform, we watch and listen carefully without interrupting the performance. When each group performs, ensure that the audience can see the actions and hear the sounds clearly.

- Display **PowerPoint Slide 4** and give students **Worksheet 7.4.1**. Read through **Activity 1** with the class so that they know what to look and listen for. Ask them to add details after each performance. Choose whether students complete the Activity 1 table for all groups, or whether they should focus on one or two groups.

- Display **PowerPoint Slide 5** and ask students to complete **Activity 2** on their worksheets. They should reflect on their own participation and the reasons for the choices they made.

Worksheet 7.4.1 — *'I pray thee, gentle mortal, sing again.'*

Activity 1

After each performance, consider:

- What emotions did the group capture?
- Which gestures and sounds did they use to do this?
- Are gestures and sounds universal? Do they mean the same for everyone?

Group names	Sounds/gestures used	What emotions did they represent?

Activity 2

- You have rehearsed and possibly even performed your scene, using only sound and movement.
- Complete the self-evaluation grid below.

The key emotions I portrayed were:		
The gestures I used were:		
The sounds I used were:		
The reasons for these choices were:		

Extract 7.4.2
Act 3 Sc 2
'Fie, fie! you counterfeit, you puppet you!'

The story continues …

Puck has got things wrong! He placed the juice from the magical flower in the wrong Athenian's eyes. Oberon tries to correct Puck's mistake and places the juice on Demetrius's eyes. Now both Lysander and Demetrius love Helena. She thinks they are playing a cruel joke and Hermia thinks Helena has stolen Lysander. They argue.

Hermia
O me! you **juggler**! you **cankerblossom**!
You thief of love! What! Have you come by night,
And stol'n my love's heart from him?

Helena
Fine, i' faith!
Have you no modesty, no maiden shame, 285
No touch of **bashfulness**? What! Will you tear
Impatient answers from my gentle tongue?
Fie, fie! you **counterfeit**, you puppet you!

Hermia
'Puppet!' why so? Ay, that way goes the game.
Now I perceive that she hath made compare 290
Between our statures; she hath urg'd her height;
And with her personage, her tall personage,
Her height, forsooth, she hath **prevail'd with him**.
And are you grown so high in his esteem
Because I am so dwarfish and so low? 295
How low am I, thou painted maypole? Speak.
How low am I? I am not yet so low
But that my nails can reach unto thine eyes.

Helena
I pray you, though you mock me, gentlemen,
Let her not hurt me. I was never **curst**; 300
I have no gift at all in **shrewishness**;
I am a right maid for my cowardice;
Let her not strike me. You perhaps may think,
Because she is something lower than myself,
That I can match her. 305

Hermia

                      'Lower' hark, again.

Helena

    Good Hermia, do not be so bitter with me.
    I evermore did love you, Hermia,
    Did ever keep your **counsels**, never wrong'd you;
    Save that, in love unto Demetrius,
    I told him of your stealth unto this wood.   310
    He followed you; for love I followed him;
    But he hath **chid me hence**, and threaten'd me
    To strike me, spurn me, nay, to kill me too;
    And now, so you will let me quiet go,
    To Athens will I bear my folly back,   315
    And follow you no further. Let me go.
    You see how simple and how fond I am.

Hermia

    Why, get you gone! Who is't that hinders you?

Helena

    A foolish heart that I leave here behind.

Hermia

    What! with Lysander?

Helena

                            With Demetrius.   320

Glossary

juggler: cheat

cankerblossom: bud-eating maggot

bashfulness: sensitive shrinking

Fie, fie!: For shame!

counterfeit: fake

prevail'd with him: won him to love her

curst: bad-tempered

shrewishness: spiteful scolding

counsels: secrets

chid me hence: driven me away angrily

Lesson 7.4.2 — *'Fie, fie! you counterfeit, you puppet you!'*

Learning objective(s):
- To understand the motivation and feelings of Hermia and Helena.
- To explore opinions through hot-seating.

Resources:
- PowerPoint 7.4.2
- Extract 7.4.2
- Worksheet 7.4.2

Recap and reflection

- Show **PowerPoint slide 1** and share the lesson objectives with the class. Then display **PowerPoint slide 2**. Revisit what students remember of the plot so far. This can be facilitated as a whole-class question and answer activity or as individual responses to be self-marked. *Answers: 1. Hermia and Lysander; 2. Demetrius; 3. Helena; 4. Lysander's; 5. Helena; 6. Demetrius's; 7. Now both men love Helena.*

Developing skills

- Get started by reading **Extract 7.4.2**. Use the recap and glossary to consolidate students' knowledge. Then allocate the parts or ask students to read in pairs.

- Display **PowerPoint slide 3**. Ask students to work in pairs to match the quotations taken from Extract 7.4.2 with their modern translation. Check students' understanding of what the characters think about each other. *Answers: 'you juggler! you cankerblossom!' = You are a cheat and a bud-eating maggot!; 'You thief of love!' = You have stolen my love away from me!; 'And with her personage, her tall personage, Her height, forsooth, she hath prevail'd with him' = You have only won Lysander because you are tall.; 'thou painted maypole' = You wear too much make-up.*

- Now repeat the activity with Helena's quotations on **PowerPoint slide 4**. *Answers: 'Have you no modesty, no maiden shame, No touch of bashfulness?' = Are you not sensitive? You have no shame or modesty; 'you counterfeit, you puppet you!' = You fake, you little doll!; 'I was never curst' = I was never bad-tempered until you came along; 'she is something lower than myself' = She is shorter than me.*

Trying it yourself

- Display **PowerPoint slide 5**. Choose two members of the group to be Helena and Hermia. These are the characters to be hot-seated. Use knowledge from the previous task to help your students understand how their character may be feeling. The rest of the group are to act as interviewers. Each member of the class should ask a question of one of the characters. The person playing that character should respond as the character might. This is a largely improvised task, so choose students who can think quickly and stay in character to be in the hotseat. If you have a large group, students can be put in teams to think of a relevant question. Some groups will need to be given ideas. *For example: Tell me how you came to be in the woods at night. What was your friendship like before you fell out over Lysander? Have you changed your mind about getting married?*

- Remind students that at the end of the process, they should be prepared to choose a side: Team Helena or Team Hermia. Prompt students by asking the final questions on the slide: 'Who do you think we should have more sympathy for?' and 'Who is more justified in feeling aggrieved?'

Final task

- Display **PowerPoint slide 6** and give students **Worksheet 7.4.2** so they can use the voting slip to cast their vote. The students playing Helena and Hermia should also vote. Count the votes to see which side has won. Ask students to discuss the reasons for their choices as part of whole-class feedback.

Taking it further

- Follow up with a reciprocal reading lesson of Act 3 pages 63 to 113 of *Collins Classroom Classics*. Or watch a version of Act 3 in its entirety, such as those available to stream online from Shakespeare's Globe Theatre, the National Theatre or the RSC.

Worksheet 7.4.2: 'Fie, fie! you counterfeit, you puppet you!'

Final task

- Use the voting slip below to cast your vote for either Helena or Hermia.
- Which character made the most persuasive argument?
- Which character do you sympathise with?
- Be prepared to justify your ideas!

VOTING SLIP	
Helena	☐
Hermia	☐

Give three reasons for voting the way you did:

1. ....
   ....

2. ....
   ....

3. ....
   ....

Extract 7.5.1
Act 4 Sc 1
'The fierce vexation of a dream'

The story continues ...
Oberon, realising the mistake Puck has made with the lovers, instructs him to create a fog and lead the lovers through the forest and then to sleep so they can put things right. Oberon sees that Titania is still in love with Nick Bottom the weaver, who is transformed to have a donkey's head.

Titania

    Sleep thou, and I will wind thee in my arms.   40
    Fairies, begone, and be all ways away.

        [Exeunt FAIRIES]

    So doth the **woodbine** the sweet **honeysuckle**
    Gently entwist; the female ivy so
    Enrings the barky fingers of the elm.
    O, how I love thee! how I dote on thee!   45

        [They sleep]

        [Enter PUCK]

Oberon [Advancing]

    Welcome, good Robin. Seest thou this sweet sight?
    Her **dotage** now I do begin to pity;
    For, meeting her of late behind the wood,
    Seeking sweet favours for this hateful fool,
    I did upbraid her and fall out with her.   50
    For she his hairy temples then had rounded
    With a coronet of fresh and fragrant flowers;
    And that same dew, which sometime on the buds
    Was wont to swell like round and orient pearls
    Stood now within the pretty flowerets' eyes,   55
    Like tears that did their own disgrace bewail.
    When I had at my pleasure taunted her
    And she in mild terms begg'd my patience,
    I then did ask of her her changeling child;
    Which straight she gave me, and her fairy sent   60
    To bear him to my bower in fairy land.
    And now I have the boy, I will undo
    This hateful imperfection of her eyes.
    And, gentle Puck, take this transformed scalp

	From off the head of this Athenian **swain**,	65
	That he awaking when the other do,	
	May all to Athens back again repair,	
	And think no more of this night's accidents	
	But as the fierce vexation of a dream.	
	But first I will release the Fairy Queen.	70

[Touching her eyes]

> Be as thou wast wont to be;
> See as thou wast wont to see.
> Dian's bud o'er Cupid's flower
> Hath such force and blessed power.

Now, my Titania; wake you, my sweet queen. 75

Titania

My Oberon! What visions have I seen!
Methought I was **enamour'd** of an ass.

Oberon

There lies your love.

Titania

How came these things to pass?
O, how mine eyes do loathe his **visage** now!

Oberon

Silence awhile. Robin, take off this head. 80
Titania, music call; and strike more dead
Than common sleep of all these five the sense.

Glossary

woodbine; honeysuckle: climbing plants

dotage: obsession

swain: workman

enamour'd: in love with

visage: face

Lesson 7.5.1 — *'The fierce vexation of a dream'*

Learning objective(s):	Resources:
• To understand the development of the plot. • To explore and create images of the natural world.	• PowerPoint 7.5.1 • Extract 7.5.1 • Worksheet 7.5.1

Getting started

- Show **PowerPoint slide 1** and share the lesson objectives with the class. Using **PowerPoint slide 2**, allow students a few minutes to think about what Oberon would need to do to bring peace and harmony back to the forest. Answers are: *1. Remove the spell from Lysander and put the potion on Demetrius's eyes to ensure that he falls in love with Helena; 2. Remove the spell from Titania; 3. Remove the donkey's head from Bottom.*

- Using **Extract 7.5.1**, read aloud **The story continues …** and then use volunteer readers for the exchange between Titania and Oberon.

Developing skills

- Ask students to work in pairs and focus on Oberon's speech. Use the questions on **PowerPoint slide 3**. Students should decide on the answers together and then write them individually in their notebooks using clear statements to answer the 'what' questions. They should support each statement with a quotation from the speech to back their response. Encourage students to develop their responses with an inference, drawing on their skills from Week 1. Answers should include that: *1. Oberon feels sorry for Titania when he sees her with the donkey/Bottom; 2. He had met her and taunted her in the woods; 3. Titania had asked him to be patient and changed her mind about the changeling boy; 4. Oberon decides to remove the spell from Titania; 5. He asks Puck to remove the donkey's head from Bottom.*

- Working with the whole class, use **PowerPoint slide 4** to draw attention to Shakespeare's use of natural imagery. Ask students to consider what impression we have of the forest from these descriptions. What do they see in their mind's eye? What is suggested by verbs and verb phrases such as 'gently entwist' and 'enrings'? How are the plants growing? How do the noun phrases appeal to our senses? Explore the two similes and discuss why the dewdrops are like tears. Recap on key subject vocabulary using the keywords on the slide. Leaving the slide in place and using **Worksheet 7.5.1**, consolidate this knowledge by asking students to work individually on **Activity 1**.

- Then ask students to continue to work individually on **Activity 2**, where they consider the idea of the magical forest. Encourage students to mind map ideas about what they might find here, drawing on the images they have just considered and expanding further. Allow some time for students to feed back, share ideas and add to their mind map. Encourage them to think about their senses, the kinds of plants that might grow there, the smells and sounds, the type of creatures and whether there would be water, starlight and moonlight, caves.

Trying it yourself

- Using **Activity 3** on the worksheet, introduce the idea that imagery is created through a combination of language 'special effects'. Ask students to work individually on **Activity 3**, drawing on ideas from their mind map to create examples of the five language 'special effects' in the grid.

Taking it further

- Follow up with a reciprocal reading lesson completing a read of Act 4 scene 1 from page 115 to 131 of the *Collins Classroom Classics*. Alternatively, students could watch a performance or film version of Act 4 scene 1 such as the ones available to stream online from Shakespeare's Globe Theatre, the National Theatre or the RSC.

Worksheet 7.5.1 — *'The fierce vexation of a dream'*

Activity 1

Select the correct examples from the slide using the definitions to help you.

Techniques to create imagery	Definition	Example
Adjective	A word that describes an object, person or place and its qualities.	
Noun phrase	An adjective or adjectives together with a noun, creating a descriptive phrase.	
Verb/verb phrase	A word or cluster of words that describe an action, the way something moves, what things do or how things are.	
Personification	Describing an object with human qualities as if it has been brought to life by magic!	
Simile	A way of describing something by comparing it to something else, using the words 'like' or 'as' to do so.	

Activity 2

In the play, all the main characters have now been in a forest where magic was at work. Create a mind map below of all the things you imagine could be found in a magical forest.

Activity 3

As well as using specific words and phrases, writers create **imagery** to help us visualise more effectively and bring their writing to life in our imaginations – almost like creating 'special effects' in a film. Using the ideas from your mind map, create some of your own **language 'special effects'** using the table below.

Language special effect	Definition	My magical forest example
Simile	A way of describing something by comparing it to something else using the words 'like' or 'as'.	
Metaphor	A way of creating an image by describing it as actually being something else, e.g.: The moon was a silver coin in the night sky.	
Personification	Describing an object with human qualities as if it has been brought to life by magic!	
Alliteration	A pattern of sounds in a description created by using words that begin with the same letter, e.g.: The **s**tars **s**parkled in a **s**ky made of **s**atin.	
Onomatopoeia	A sound effect where you use a word to represent the noise you want to describe, e.g.: The owl **hooted** a warning to the sleeping woodland.	

Extract 7.5.2
Act 4 Sc 1

'It seems to me that yet we sleep, we dream.'

The story continues ...

Theseus and Hippolyta, accompanied by their servants and Egeus, arrive in the forest for an early morning hunt. They discover the four lovers sleeping in the forest. Egeus is outraged when Lysander confesses that he and Hermia were eloping. However, Oberon's magic has set things right and Demetrius explains that he now loves and wishes to marry Helena. Theseus overrules Egeus and decrees that the couples can marry: Demetrius and Helena, Lysander and Hermia.

Demetrius
These things seem small and undistinguishable,
Like far-off mountains turned into clouds.

Hermia
Methinks I see these things with **parted eye**,
When every thing seems double.

Helena
                              So methinks;   190
And I have found Demetrius like a jewel,
Mine own, and not mine own.

Demetrius
                              Are you sure
That we are awake? It seems to me
That yet we sleep, we dream. Do not you think
The Duke was here, and bid us follow him?   195

Hermia
Yea, and my father.

Helena
                              And Hippolyta.

Lysander
And he did bid us follow to the temple.

Demetrius
Why, then, we are awake; let's follow him;
And by the way let us recount our dreams.

[*Exeunt*]

Bottom [Awaking]

When my cue comes, call me, and I will answer. My next is 'Most fair Pyramus.' Heigh-ho! Peter Quince! Flute, the bellows-mender! Snout, the tinker! Starveling! God's my life, stol'n hence, and left me asleep! I have had a most rare vision. I have had a dream, past the wit of man to say what dream it was. Man is but an ass, if he go about to **expound** this dream. Methought I was – there is no man can tell what. Methought I was, and methought I had, but man is but a **patch'd fool**, if he will offer to say what methought I had. The eye of man hath not heard, the ear of man hath not seen, man's hand is not able to taste, his tongue to conceive, nor his heart to report, what my dream was. I will get Peter Quince to write a ballad of this dream. It shall be call'd 'Bottom's Dream,' because it hath no bottom; and I will sing it in the latter end of a play, before the Duke. **Peradventure**, to make it the more gracious, I shall sing it at her death.

Glossary

parted eye: double vision

expound: explain

patch'd fool: a clown or jester

peradventure: perhaps

Lesson 7.5.2 — 'It seems to me that yet we sleep, we dream.'

Learning objective(s):
- To plan and write a description based on a picture.
- To use imagery to bring a description to life.

Resources:
- PowerPoint 7.5.2
- Extract 7.5.2
- Worksheet 7.5.2

Recap and reflection

- Show **PowerPoint slide 1** and share the lesson objectives with the class. Read aloud **The story continues …** on **Extract 7.5.2**, then allocate students to read aloud from the end of Act 4 Scene 1 where the lovers and Bottom awake from their 'dreams'. Working with the whole group, lead into a discussion exploring the lovers' perceptions and feelings at this point. Why are they so confused? What have they just heard Theseus confirm? Can they believe the situation? Who do the students think would be most surprised at this outcome? Who do they think would be most relieved?

- Reflect with students on the idea of the magical forest. Who has been asleep in the forest? Who has had a dream? What has caused some of the characters to sleep and to wake? What changes have they experienced? Reflect on how the forest/the natural world was under the control of the fairy world and specifically the Fairy King and Queen. What impact have they had? Are the rules of the fairy world different from reality, or do they have things in common? You might like to reflect on the roles of Theseus/Oberon compared with Hippolyta/Titania, for example. What did students imagine in lesson 7.5.1 about the qualities of a magical forest?

Developing skills

- Display **PowerPoint slide 2** showing an image of a magical forest and the task students are to work on. Distribute **Worksheet 7.5.2** and ask students to look carefully at the image on the slide for one minute, noting the order in which their eye takes in five main details from the image. Then ask them to complete the first column of their planning grid. Each detail will become the focus of a single paragraph.

- Use **PowerPoint slide 3** to model a possible outcome for this and explain the idea of the topic sentence: a clear introductory statement sentence that sets up the focus for each paragraph. Allow time for students to create a topic sentence for each of their paragraphs.

- Use **PowerPoint slide 4** to remind students of the palette of language techniques they have at their disposal to enable them to create imagery. Students may wish to draw on the images they created in lesson 7.5.1. Use this opportunity to check and consolidate that students can remember what each of these techniques are. If time allows, invite some students to share their creations from lesson 7.5.1.

- Ask students to work in pairs on **Activity 2** on **Worksheet 7.5.2**, confirming that they can recognise and identify the different language techniques in the model paragraph. Use **PowerPoint slide 5** with the whole group to check findings and take suggestions. Students should have picked up on: *noun phrases, interesting verbs, personification, a simile and a metaphor*. Establish that you would like students' own paragraphs to aim to use descriptive language techniques in a similar way. Encourage students to see how this model paragraph leads towards the topic of paragraph 2 on the model plan on slide 3.

Final task

- Display **PowerPoint slide 2** again and allow time for students to write up their five-paragraph description. Reinforce that the success criteria include keeping a single focus in each paragraph and that you are looking for them to create imagery in each paragraph using the techniques from the palette and from the previous lesson. Encourage students to use their imagination to bring the image of the forest to life and include as many magical elements as they wish. This task may also include homework time.

Taking it further

- Follow up with a reciprocal reading lesson completing a read of Act 4 Scene 2 from page 131 to 135 of the *Collins Classroom Classics*. Alternatively, watch the remainder of Act 4 and the performance of Pyramus and Thisbe from a version of the play in performance such as the ones available to stream online from Shakespeare's Globe Theatre, the National Theatre or the RSC.

Worksheet 7.5.2 — *'It seems to me that yet we sleep, we dream.'*

Activity 1

You are going to plan and write a description of a magical forest based on the picture on the slide. Pay attention to the order in which your eye takes in all the details in the image.

1. Use the planning grid below to list those details in order. Each detail is going to be the focus of a single paragraph in your description, so write them in the first column of the grid.
2. When you are ready, go on to write a clear topic sentence for each paragraph, thinking about the language techniques to create imagery that you have learned about during the last lesson. Write this in the second column in the grid.

Detail from the picture	Topic sentence
Paragraph 1:	
Paragraph 2:	
Paragraph 3:	
Paragraph 4:	
Paragraph 5:	

Activity 2

How many different descriptive language features can you find in the model paragraph?

The crystal clear water danced and sang down the rocky steps. Bubbles of air chuckled happily in the early morning sunlight as if a fairy was swimming and frolicking in the gurgling stream. As the waterfall cascaded over the ancient stones, sunlight bounced on the surface, creating rainbows of light before it reached its destination.

Extract 7.6.1
Act 2 Sc 1
'The poet's eye ... Doth glance from heaven to earth'

The story continues …

The action shifts to Theseus and Hippolyta's wedding day, where they are joined by the four lovers who are now also happily married. Theseus calls for some entertainment and the Mechanicals have the chance to show their performance of Pyramus and Thisbe. When the play is over and everyone is sleeping, the fairies return to bless the couples and their futures together.

Titania

These are the forgeries of jealousy;
And never, since the middle summer's spring,
Met we on hill, in dale, forest, or **mead**,
By paved fountain, or by rushy brook,
Or in the beached **margent** of the sea,   85
To dance our **ringlets** to the whistling wind,
But with thy brawls thou hast disturb'd our sport.
Therefore the winds, piping to us in vain,
As in revenge, have suck'd up from the sea
Contagious fogs; which, falling in the land,   90
Have every pelting river made so proud
That they have overborne their continents.
The ox hath therefore stretch'd his yoke in vain,
The ploughman lost his sweat, and the green corn
Hath rotted ere his youth attain'd a beard;   95
The fold stands empty in the drowned field,
And crows are fatted with the **murrion** flock;
The **nine men's morris** is fill'd up with mud,
And the quaint mazes in the wanton green,
For lack of tread, are undistinguishable.   100
The human mortals want their winter here;
No night is now with hymn or carol blest;
Therefore the moon, the governess of floods,
Pale in her anger, washes all the air,
That **rheumatic diseases** do abound.   105
And thorough this distemperature we see
The seasons alter: hoary-headed frosts
Fall in the fresh lap of the crimson rose;
And on **old Hiems'** thin and icy crown

An odorous chaplet of sweet summer buds 110
Is, as in mockery, set. The spring, the summer,
The childing autumn, angry winter, change
Their **wonted liveries**; and the mazed world,
By their increase, now knows not which is which.
And this same **progeny** of evils comes 115
From our debate, from our dissension;
We are their parents and original.

Glossary

mead: meadow

margent: the edge or margins

ringlets: dancing in a circle

murrion: diseased

nine men's morris: an outdoor game cut into the grass

rheumatic diseases: coughs and colds

old Hiem: winter

wonted liveries: their usual clothes

progeny: offspring or brood

Lesson 7.6.1

'The poet's eye ... Doth glance from heaven to earth'

Learning objective(s):
- To explore Shakespeare's possible message or intentions.
- To make contextual connections between the themes of the play and environmental issues today.

Resources:
- PowerPoint 7.6.1
- Extract 7.6.1
- Worksheet 7.6.1

Getting started

- Show **PowerPoint slide 1** and share the objectives with the class. Display **PowerPoint slide 2** and, with the whole group, explore the two prompt questions. Take suggestions for the first question and then read aloud the short extract from Theseus's speech from Act 5 Scene 1. Aim for students to understand that Shakespeare was a poet and a playwright. Prompt them to think about this view of what a poet does. How is a writer able to bring things to life from their imagination? You might like to reflect on students' own creative writing linked to Act 4 and the creation of imagery. Prompt students to think about whether writers just write about '*airy nothing*'. Lead students to think about the ideas in the play and if they are still relevant for us today.

- Distribute **Worksheet 7.6.1** and ask students to work in pairs on **Activity 1**. Recap or introduce the idea of 'theme' and ask students to identify the 'big ideas' or themes from the play. Suggested responses might include: *love; dreams; magic; nature; relationships*; *conflict*.

Developing skills

- Using **Extract 7.6.1** and **PowerPoint slide 3** invite students to recap earlier in the play when we witnessed the conflict between Titania and Oberon and the impact this had on the natural world. Read the extract aloud or play an audio or video version of the speech (at the time of publication a number are available online).

- Working in pairs, or small groups for more support, ask students to annotate the speech, identifying the problems that have been caused in the natural world. Then ask them to note down if any of these issues are problematic in our world today. In a plenary, invite students to share the ideas they've identified and their suggestions, working through the speech with the class to consolidate understanding.

- Now ask students to work in small groups on **Activity 2** on the worksheet, which links to the images on **PowerPoint slides 4–6**. You could appoint a scribe to collate the group's notes and ideas. Allow groups enough time to explore the images using the prompt questions on the worksheet. They should be able to make links between the issues Titania has pointed out and similar issues in our natural world today, for example: *1. The idea of crops dying from heat or disease has an impact on the food we are able to produce; extreme weather suggests the power of the natural world and how we are unable to control it. 2. The image of the flooding is a reminder of the impact of damage to our environment – students may make cross-curricular links to their geography work; the image of the woman in the mask reminds us of contagious disease and how viruses can cause chaos and devastation. 3. The final two images remind us of the issues connected to climate change, the idea of the seasons being out of balance and the concerns this raises for the natural world.*

Trying it yourself

- Using the outcomes of their group discussion for Activity 2, ask students to complete **Activity 3** on the worksheet individually, reflecting on the themes and ideas discussed in the lesson. Allow students some time to consider the statements, reminding them of earlier lessons concerning the belief in fairies/magic; the conflict in the fairy world and its impact; the lovers and the Mechanicals and what happened to them in the forest – what they were and were not aware of; the outcomes of the spells that were used on the lovers.

Worksheet 7.6.1

'The poet's eye ... Doth glance from heaven to earth'

Activity 1

A **theme** is a 'big idea' in a play and it is important all the way through. What do you think are some of the main **themes** or 'big ideas' in *A Midsummer Night's Dream*? Make a list here.

....

....

....

....

Are any of the **themes** you have noted down relevant for us today? If so, in what ways?

....

....

....

....

Activity 2

In small groups, explore the following images, which are also shown on the PowerPoint slides. In your groups, note down your thoughts and feelings and what you can infer as you think about the following questions.

1. What is happening in the natural world in these images? How do they link to Titania's speech (which Shakespeare wrote over 400 years ago)? What do they tell us about how we should look after and respect the natural world? What is worrying about the image of the crops dying?

2. What dangers and risks do these images highlight? How do they link to Titania's speech? What does the image of the street make you feel? Are some areas of the world more at risk from serious problems because we don't all take care of our planet? What things in the natural world can affect our health and make us ill?

3. What issues or concerns do these images remind us of? How does this link to Titania's speech? What do we know about what is happening to the seasons and the weather on our planet? As a young person, how do you feel about this? What are the different views and thoughts of your group?

Activity 3

Which of these statements do you most agree with? Write 2–3 sentences explaining your choice.

1. Shakespeare's play was written over 400 years ago, but it can still remind us that the natural world is 'magical'.
2. Shakespeare's play reminds us that problems, conflicts and chaos can occur when we don't respect the natural world.
3. Shakespeare's play shows us that humans are too busy with their own concerns to notice what is happening in the natural world.
4. Shakespeare's play shows us that the natural world is powerful and can control our lives more than we sometimes realise.

....

....

....

© HarperCollins*Publishers* Ltd 2022   44   Year 7, *A Midsummer Night's Dream*, Week 6

Lesson 7.6.2

'And thorough this distemperature we see the seasons alter'

Learning objective(s):
- To recap basic persuasive techniques.
- To plan and write a short speech reflecting on the theme of the natural world.

Resources:
- PowerPoint 7.6.2
- Worksheet 7.6.2

Recap and reflection

- Recap the previous lesson by sharing some of the thoughts and outcomes of Activity 3 in which students considered the play's possible message for us as contemporary audiences/readers. Show **PowerPoint slide 1** and share the lesson objectives with the class.

- Display **PowerPoint slide 2** and see if students recognise the young campaigner Greta Thunberg. Let students know that she has made several speeches in places of influence to campaign to protect the planet from climate change. If time allows, listen to one of those speeches. At the time of publication, a number of these are available to watch online. Introduce the idea of the power of speech-making for presenting a point of view. Suggest how the power of speech-making is one that young campaigners can use to great effect.

Developing skills

- Use **PowerPoint slides 3 and 4** to introduce or recap basic persuasive techniques. Distribute **Worksheet 7.6.2** and allow students to consolidate their knowledge by completing the multiple-choice questions in **Activity 1**. Answers are: *1b; 2a; 3c; 4a; 5a.*

Final task

- Introduce the final speech-writing task, **Activity 2** on the worksheet. Unpack the nature of the statement with students: Is the task referring to real 'magic' or is this a metaphor? What might this mean about our world? What aspects of our natural world can be magical? Encourage students to think more broadly about the world beyond school to consider the seasons and what happens in each of them; the seas and the varieties of creatures within; the many different species we share our planet with; the rich variety of plants; how trees produce the oxygen we breathe and the role of bees as pollinators. Ask students to draw on their cross-curricular knowledge.

- Allow students planning time for their piece of writing using the grid on the worksheet. If facilities are available, allow students the opportunity to research their topic, perhaps using the websites of some of the key charities involved in protecting the environment where they may also see persuasive techniques in action.

- Allow time for students to complete their written speech. This could also be completed as a homework task to allow for more research time.

Taking it further

- Create space for a 'model' conference where students can formally present their prepared speeches to the class.

- Finish with a reciprocal reading lesson, completing a read of Act 5 from page 137 to page 169 in *Collins Classroom Classics*. Students may enjoy taking on the roles of the Mechanicals in a fun performance of *Pyramus and Thisbe*, with the remainder of the class as audience and the wedding party.

Worksheet 7.6.2

'And thorough this distemperature we see the seasons alter'

Activity 1

Complete the multiple-choice questions below to recap the key techniques to use in persuasive tasks.

1. Which of the following sentences contains a **shocking statistic**?

    a) The polar ice caps are melting. ☐

    b) Sea levels have risen by approximately 20 centimetres in the past eight years. ☐

    c) We must protect the bee population. ☐

2. Which of the following contains an example of **direct address**?

    a) You are the generation who must act now. ☐

    b) In years to come, we might regret not acting now. ☐

    c) I really want to get something done about climate change. ☐

3. Which of the following is an example of **factual information**?

    a) Some people think that the scientists are wrong. ☐

    b) In my opinion, we are too late to repair the damage to the planet. ☐

    c) Fossil fuels are things like coal, gas and oil. ☐

4. Which of the following is an example of a **command**?

    a) Take action right now. ☐

    b) There is no time to lose. ☐

    c) Where will we be in ten years' time? ☐

5. Which of the following might be considered **emotive**?

    a) So much of our wildlife is getting confused by warmer winters and early springs. ☐

    b) How can you reduce the amount of plastic in your household? ☐

    c) Bigger storms may cause flooding. ☐

Activity 2

You have been invited to a Young People's Conference about protecting the environment we live in.

You have been asked to make a short speech at this conference on this topic:

Our natural world is filled with magic. It is up to us to protect and take care of it.

- Begin by completing the planning grid below to organise your ideas.
- Organise your speech into five paragraphs, each one dealing with a separate idea.
- Make use of clear topic sentences.
- Include a persuasive technique in each paragraph.
- Conclude with a request or 'call to action' for your listeners.

Planning questions	Notes and planning
Who will hear my speech? Should I be formal or informal?	
First line for impact: How will I get everyone's attention straight away?	
Persuasive idea 1: Key technique to include	
Persuasive idea 2: Key technique to include	
Persuasive idea 3: Key technique to include	
What is my idea for a possible solution? What will be my request or 'call to action' for my listeners?	

Extract 8.1.1 Act 1 Sc 1

'My purse, my person, my extremest means, Lie all unlock'd to your occasions'

The story so far ...

Antonio is a wealthy merchant in the city of Venice with all his ships at sea trading in goods. However, he is unhappy and depressed at the start of the play. His friends try to cheer him up but to no avail. His close friend Bassanio arrives. He is a younger, more reckless man, who has wasted his own fortune and owes Antonio a great deal of money. He comes to tell Antonio of a new love and a plan to improve his fortunes.

Antonio
 Well; tell me now what lady is the same
 To whom you swore a secret pilgrimage,   120
 That you to-day promis'd to tell me of?

Bassanio
 'Tis not unknown to you, Antonio,
 How much I have **disabled mine estate**
 By something showing a more swelling port
 Than my faint means would grant continuance;   125
 Nor do I now make moan to be abridg'd
 From such a noble rate; but my chief care
 Is to come fairly off from the great debts
 Wherein my time, something too prodigal,
 Hath left me **gag'd**. To you, Antonio,   130
 I owe the most, in money and in love;
 And from your love I have a warranty
 To unburden all my plots and purposes
 How to get clear of all the debts I owe.

Antonio
 I pray you, good Bassanio, let me know it;   135
 And if it stand, as you yourself still do,
 Within the eye of honour, be assur'd
 My purse, my person, my extremest means,
 Lie all unlock'd to your occasions.

Bassanio
 In my school-days, when I had lost one **shaft**,   140
 I shot his fellow of the self-same flight
 The self-same way, with more advised watch,
 To find the other forth; and by adventuring both
 I oft found both. I urge this childhood proof,
 Because what follows is pure innocence.   145
 I owe you much; and, like a wilful youth,
 That which I owe is lost; but if you please
 To shoot another arrow that self way
 Which you did shoot the first, I do not doubt,

	As I will watch the aim, or to find both,	150
	Or bring your latter hazard back again	
	And thankfully rest debtor for the first.	

Antonio

You know me well, and herein spend but time
To wind about my love with circumstance;
And out of doubt you do me now more wrong   155
In making question of my uttermost
Than if you had made waste of all I have.
Then do but say to me what I should do
That in your knowledge may by me be done,
And I am **prest unto it**; therefore, speak.   160

Bassanio

In Belmont is a lady richly left,
And she is fair and, fairer than that word,
Of wondrous virtues. Sometimes from her eyes
I did receive fair speechless messages.
Her name is Portia – nothing undervalu'd   165
To Cato's daughter, Brutus' Portia.
Nor is the wide world ignorant of her worth;
For the four winds blow in from every coast
Renowned suitors, and her sunny locks
Hang on her temples like a golden fleece,   170
Which makes her seat of Belmont **Colchos' strond,
And many Jasons come in quest of her**.
O my Antonio, had I but the means
To hold a rival place with one of them,
I have a mind presages me such thrift   175
That I should questionless be fortunate.

Antonio

Thou know'st that all my fortunes are at sea;
Neither have I money nor commodity
To raise a present sum; therefore go forth,
Try what my credit can in Venice do;   180
That shall be rack'd, even to the uttermost,
To furnish thee to Belmont to fair Portia.
Go presently inquire, and so will I,
Where money is; and I no question make
To have it of my trust or for my sake.   185

[Exeunt.]

Glossary

disabled mine estate: damaged my wealth
gag'd: owing money
shaft: arrow
prest unto it: ready to help
Colchos' strond, And many Jasons come in quest of her: a reference to Jason and the Argonauts from Greek mythology and the place where Jason searched for a golden fleece

Lesson 8.1.1

'My purse, my person, my extremest means, Lie all unlock'd to your occasions'

Learning objective(s):	Resources:
• To understand the characters of Bassanio and Antonio. • To introduce Portia and her situation.	• PowerPoint 8.1.1 • Extract 8.1.1 • Worksheet 8.1.1

Sensitivity note: This play handles themes of prejudice towards peoples of Jewish faith and culture, and uses the term 'Jew' in a derogatory manner. Please handle these themes sensitively and consider setting ground rules for how your class can discuss this respectfully.

Getting started

- Share the lesson objectives on **PowerPoint slide 1** with the class. Display **PowerPoint slide 2** showing the image of Venice. Ask students what they notice about the buildings, the architecture, and the landscape. Does this seem to be a wealthy place, or a place steeped in poverty? This is a contemporary image, but what does it tell us about the buildings? What do students notice about the 'streets' of Venice? Display **PowerPoint slide 3** showing the map of Renaissance Italy and the explanatory text.

- Zoom in on the location of Venice. What is interesting about its location between the West and the East? Why might this be a good location for trade and merchants in times gone by? Prompt students to think about how great wealth might be made from the East in terms of spices, fabrics and jewels. Explain that the play is set against this backdrop, and we are about to meet its characters.

- Distribute **Extract 8.1.1** and read out **The story so far ...** Ask two confident readers to read the extract aloud for the class, taking the roles of Antonio and Bassanio.

Developing skills

- Display **PowerPoint slide 4** and ask students to work in pairs to explore the extract in relation to the four questions, making notes of their responses in their notebook. Allow a little time for pairs to feed back their findings, which should include: *Bassanio has lost his own money and has had to cut back on his lifestyle; he owes Antonio money; he has a plan to clear his debts; he seems to be a carefree and perhaps reckless character; we question what he has wasted his money on; Antonio seems perhaps a little gullible; Antonio is still keen to lend Bassanio money and help him, and he seems willing to borrow money himself to do so.*

- Hand out **Worksheet 8.1.1** and ask students to work individually on **Activity 1**, writing their answers in their notebooks. Ensure that they use the clear comprehension method outlined in the bullet points so that they produce their responses in a clear and organised way.

- Organise students into small discussion groups to complete **Activity 2**. Allow them time to discuss and make notes on the prompt questions and explore the short extract before feeding back. Suggested responses might include that: *Portia is very wealthy and very beautiful and is attracting many suitors from many different places; Bassanio feels she has shown an interest in him.* Encourage students to consider the moral implication of Bassanio wanting to make use of Portia's fortune to clear his debts. Also encourage them to note that an obstacle is the fact that Portia cannot choose her own husband and that her father has set in place a test for would-be suitors described as a 'lottery'.

- Display **PowerPoint slide 5** showing an artist's impression of Portia's Belmont estate. Take suggestions as to the contrast between this image and the earlier impressions of Venice. Draw attention to the fact that this is secluded, perhaps in the countryside, away from the hustle and bustle of the busy port city. What impression might this give of the extent of Portia's wealth?

- Use **PowerPoint slide 6** to develop and consolidate ideas from across the whole lesson. Push students to consider the motives of the characters and how ethical or altruistic they may or may not be. You might introduce the idea of the gender divide here: that Nerissa and Portia are in the private, secluded location of the Belmont estate, while the wealthy men and merchants occupy the busy trading port. Suggest how this might help us to understand how Bassanio has been distracted to spend his fortune.

Trying it yourself

- Follow up with a reciprocal reading lesson of Act 1 Scenes 2 and 3 (page 17) up to the entrance of Antonio on page 29 of *Collins Classroom Classics*.

Worksheet 8.1.1

'My purse, my person, my extremest means, Lie all unlock'd to your occasions'

Activity 1

Using the knowledge you have gained from your paired exploration, answer the following questions.

a) What do we learn from this extract about the character of Bassanio?

b) What impression is created of the character of Antonio?

Make sure you:

- use clear statement sentences in response to the task
- support your statement with a quotation from the extract
- show your interpretation of each character by making inferences. You can introduce these with stems such as: *This suggests that ...; This implies that ...; We can infer that ... .*

Activity 2

1. What have we learned about Portia from Bassanio's conversation with Antonio?
2. Why does Bassanio feel that Portia is attracted to him?
3. Why is Bassanio attracted to Portia? How do you feel about his motives for seeking her hand in marriage?
4. Now read the extract below, from Act 1 Scene 2, where we meet Portia in conversation with her maid and companion. List three things we learn about her situation.
5. What challenge has been set by Portia's father before his death?

Portia

    [...] I may neither choose who I would nor refuse
    who I dislike; so is the will of a living daughter curb'd
    by the will of a dead father. Is it not hard, Nerissa, that
    I cannot choose one, nor refuse none?   25

Nerissa

    Your father was ever virtuous, and holy men at their
    death have good inspirations; therefore the lott'ry that
    he hath devised in these three chests, of gold, silver,
    and lead – whereof who chooses his meaning chooses
    you – will no doubt never be chosen by any rightly but   30
    one who you shall rightly love. But what warmth is
    there in your affection towards any of these princely
    suitors that are already come?

Extract 8.1.2
Act 1 Sc 3
'For suff'rance is the badge of all our tribe'

The story continues ...

In Belmont, Portia is relieved that many of her suitors have left without taking her father's test. Nerissa reminds her of a young Venetian soldier who once visited Belmont, and Portia immediately remembers Bassanio's name. She is told that the Prince of Morocco is on his way to visit her. She reacts with prejudice to the fact that he is North African. Meanwhile, Bassanio and Antonio visit Shylock, a moneylender, who is of Jewish faith. Antonio asks for a loan until his ships return to enable him to support Bassanio with his plan. In this exchange, more disturbing prejudice emerges.

[Enter ANTONIO.]

Bassanio
    This is Signior Antonio. 35

Shylock
    [Aside] How like a **fawning publican** he looks!
    I hate him for he is a Christian;
    But more for that in low simplicity
    He lends out money **gratis**, and brings down
    The rate of **usance** here with us in Venice. 40
    If I can catch him once upon the hip,
    I will feed fat the ancient grudge I bear him.
    He hates our sacred nation; and he rails,
    Even there where merchants most do congregate,
    On me, my bargains, and my well-won thrift, 45
    Which he calls interest. Cursed be my tribe
    If I forgive him!

Bassanio
    Shylock, do you hear?

Shylock
    I am debating of my present store,
    And, by the near guess of my memory,
    I cannot instantly raise up the gross 50
    Of full three thousand ducats. What of that?
    Tubal, a wealthy Hebrew of my tribe,
    Will furnish me. But soft! how many months
    Do you desire? *[To ANTONIO]* Rest you fair, good signior;
    Your worship was the last man in our mouths. 55

Antonio
    Shylock, albeit I neither lend nor borrow
    By taking nor by giving of excess,
    Yet, to supply the ripe wants of my friend,

| | I'll break a custom. *[To BASSANIO]* Is he yet possess'd | |
| | How much ye would? | |

Shylock

                                      Ay, ay, three thousand ducats.   60

Antonio

   And for three months.

                        [...]

Shylock

   Three thousand ducats – 'tis a good round sum.
   Three months from twelve; then let me see, the rate –

Antonio

   Well, Shylock, shall we be beholding to you?   100

Shylock

   Signior Antonio, many a time and oft
   In the Rialto you have rated me
   About my moneys and my usances;
   Still have I borne it with a patient shrug,
   For suff'rance is the badge of all our tribe;   105
   You call me misbeliever, cut-throat dog,
   And spit upon my Jewish **gaberdine**,
   And all for use of that which is mine own.
   Well then, it now appears you need my help;
   Go to, then; you come to me, and you say   110
   'Shylock, we would have moneys'. You say so –
   You, that did **void your rheum** upon my beard
   And **foot me as you spurn a stranger cur**
   Over your threshold; moneys is your suit.
   What should I say to you? Should I not say   115
   'Hath a dog money? Is it possible
   A cur can lend three thousand ducats?' Or
   Shall I bend low and, in a bondman's key,
   With bated breath and whisp'ring humbleness,
   Say this: 120
   'Fair sir, you spit on me on Wednesday last,
   You spurn'd me such a day; another time
   You call'd me dog; and for these courtesies
   I'll lend you thus much moneys'?

Antonio

   I am as like to call thee so again,   125
   To spit on thee again, to spurn thee too.
   If thou wilt lend this money, lend it not
   As to thy friends – for when did friendship take
   A breed for barren metal of his friend? –
   But lend it rather to thine enemy,   130
   Who if he break thou mayst with better face
   Exact the penalty.

Shylock

> Why, look you, how you storm!
> I would be friends with you, and have your love,
> Forget the shames that you have stain'd me with,   135
> Supply your present wants, and take no **doit**
> Of usance for my moneys, and you'll not hear me.
> This is kind I offer.

Bassanio

> This were kindness.

Shylock

>   This kindness will I show.
> Go with me to a notary, seal me there   140
> Your single bond, and, in a merry sport,
> If you repay me not on such a day,
> In such a place, such sum or sums as are
> Express'd in the condition, let the forfeit
> Be nominated for an equal pound   145
> Of your fair flesh, to be cut off and taken
> In what part of your body pleaseth me.

Antonio

> Content, in faith; I'll seal to such a bond
> And say there is much kindness in the Jew.

Bassanio

> You shall not seal to such a bond for me;   150
> I'll rather dwell in my necessity.

Antonio

> Why, fear not, man; I will not forfeit it;
> Within these two months – that's a month before
> This bond expires – I do expect return
> Of thrice three times the value of this bond.   155

Glossary

fawning publican: a public servant looking to win favour; obsequious

gratis: for free; without interest

usance: money lending

gaberdine: a coat or cape

void your rheum: spit phlegm

foot me as you spurn a stranger cur: kick me like a stray dog

doit: a small coin

Lesson 8.1.2 — *'For suff'rance is the badge of all our tribe'*

Learning objective(s):	Resources:
• To introduce Shylock and develop our understanding of key characters. • To introduce the theme of prejudice.	• PowerPoint 8.1.2 • Extract 8.1.2 • Worksheet 8.1.2

Sensitivity note: This play handles themes of prejudice towards peoples of Jewish faith and culture, and uses the term 'Jew' in a derogatory manner. Please handle these themes sensitively and consider setting ground rules for how your class can discuss this respectfully.

Recap and reflection

- Distribute **Extract 8.1.2** and recap the previous lesson by reading **The story continues …**. Appoint three readers to take on the roles of Antonio, Bassanio and Shylock. Explore students' first impressions of this scene and the new character we have been introduced to. What divisions and prejudices seem to be at work in this cosmopolitan trading city?

- Share the lesson objectives on **PowerPoint slide 1** with the class, then display the image on **PowerPoint slide 2.** How might this image add to students' initial impressions? Who do they feel the most sympathy for here? Who looks the most vulnerable? What is interesting about the way the artist has portrayed Shylock? What do they feel is conveyed in the faces of Antonio and Bassanio in the painting?

Developing skills

- Distribute **Worksheet 8.1.2** and organise the class into small groups. Use the information at the top of the worksheet to consolidate ideas from the previous discussion. Prompt students to consider why this disparity in the law might be the cause of resentment or prejudice.

- Ask students to work in their groups to complete **Activity 1**, where the questions move students chronologically through the extract. Encourage students to discuss and then note down their collaborative answers in their notebooks. Allow some time to take feedback from different groups.

- After taking feedback, show **PowerPoint slide 3** to consolidate, gauging students' reactions to their group exploration. How does what we have witnessed open up a theme of justice in the play? Does this seem like a fair and just society?

- Use the three prompt questions on the slide to generate viewpoints. Suggested responses might include that: *Shylock hates Antonio because he belongs to a different religion, he lends money for free, which is damaging to Shylock's profession, he has been offensive to Shylock; Antonio does not believe in borrowing money but seems willing to do it for Bassanio. He may be protective of him or have a close bond with him; Shylock tells us of the terrible prejudice and treatment he has received, including offensive names and being spat upon – it shows us a much darker side to Venice and a different side to the supposed noblemen there; Shylock uses the names he has been called to ask how he is then capable of lending Antonio money now that he is in need; Antonio continues to be offensive and seems to assume that Shylock should lend him the money no matter how he treats Shylock, as this is a business transaction; Shylock's earlier aside suggests he may be seeking vengeance for his treatment by Antonio.*

Trying it yourself

- Now ask students to work individually on **Activity 2** of **Worksheet 8.1.2**. Read aloud the short extract of Shylock's speech for students and present the task. Students should use the template on the worksheet to show their understanding of the terms Shylock is asking for. Encourage students to use an appropriate register – perhaps highly formal or mirroring Shakespeare's language – to create their 'contract', which they could complete with flourishing signatures.

- Return to **PowerPoint slide 3**. In the light of Shylock's contract with Antonio, do we see a different side to these characters? How do they respond to the terms of the bond? Is this fair or just? Have the scales shifted more evenly? Who, now, is perhaps the most vulnerable and why?

Final task

- Show **PowerPoint slide 4** and work with the whole group to consider Bassanio's reaction to Shylock's deal. Ask students to suggest why he might now want Antonio to make this contract on his behalf. In what situation does it place Antonio? What does it leave Bassanio feeling responsible for? Does this show a better side to Bassanio? What is Antonio's reaction? How do students feel about his confident assertion? How does Shakespeare introduce an element of jeopardy here through this foreshadowing?

Worksheet 8.1.2 — 'For suff'rance is the badge of all our tribe'

Today, if people need to borrow large sums of money – perhaps to buy a house or a car – they are likely to go to a bank. However, in Shakespeare's time, Christians were not allowed to lend money and charge interest in order to profit from it.

We see a tension in the text between Antonio, who is of the Christian faith, and Shylock, who is of the Jewish faith. In Venice, Jewish people were allowed to lend money and charge interest, just like banks do today. They faced much prejudice in Venetian society.

We begin to see the extent of the prejudice and double standards at work in the play.

Activity 1

1. In Shylock's opening aside, what are some of the reasons he has to hate Antonio? Does this come as a surprise to you? Does this contrast with our impression of Antonio from Lesson 8.1.1?
2. What do we understand about Antonio from this speech?

> Shylock, albeit I neither lend nor borrow
> By taking nor by giving of excess,
> Yet, to supply the ripe wants of my friend,
> I'll break a custom.

What possible reasons might Antonio have for being so supportive of Bassanio?

3. Look closely at Shylock's long speech beginning '*Signior Antonio ...*'. What does he tell us about the way he has been treated by Antonio in the past? How do you respond to this? What does this show us about the supposed civilised society of Venice?
4. What does Shylock imply when he says the following to Antonio:

> Should I not say
> 'Hath a dog money? Is it possible
> A cur can lend three thousand ducats?'

What is Antonio's reaction to the point Shylock makes in the extract above? How do you respond to this?

5. When Shylock says, '*I would be friends with you, and have your love,*' do you think he is being genuine or not? Explain the reason for your choice.

Activity 2

Look at the speech below, in which Shylock sets out the terms by which he will lend Antonio the money he wants.

Imagine you are the 'notary' or lawyer that Shylock and Antonio go to see.

Design and draw up the contract between Shylock and Antonio for the loan.

>   This kindness will I show.
> Go with me to a notary, seal me there   140
> Your single bond, and, in a merry sport,
> If you repay me not on such a day,
> In such a place, such sum or sums as are
> Express'd in the condition, let the forfeit
> Be nominated for an equal pound   145
> Of your fair flesh, to be cut off and taken
> In what part of your body pleaseth me.

Drawn up in this day of our Lord: ....

In the city of Venice

Between: ....

THE FOLLOWING LEGAL AND BINDING CONTRACT

....

....

....

....

....

....

Signed: ....

Signed: ....

In the presence of: ....

Extract 8.2.1 Act 2 Sc 7 — *'All that glisters is not gold'*

The story continues ...

In Belmont, the Prince of Morocco arrives to take the test to win Portia's hand. He is keen to show his bravery, worthiness and wealth. He takes a formal oath, a condition of Portia's father, that if he fails the test, he cannot ask for anyone else's hand in marriage ever again. He must choose between three caskets of gold, silver and lead.

Belmont. Portia's house.

[Flourish of Cornets. Enter PORTIA, *with the* PRINCE OF MOROCCO, *and their Trains.]*

Portia
Go draw aside the curtains and discover
The several caskets to this noble Prince.
Now make your choice.

Morocco
The first, of gold, who this inscription bears:
'Who chooseth me shall gain what many men desire'.　　　5
The second, silver, which this promise carries:
'Who chooseth me shall get as much as he deserves'.
This third, dull lead, with warning all as blunt:
'Who chooseth me must give and hazard all he hath'.
How shall I know if I do choose the right?　　　10

Portia
The one of them contains my picture, Prince;
If you choose that, then I am yours withal.

[... After much deliberation, the Prince makes his choice.]

Portia
There, take it, Prince, and if my form lie there,　　　61
Then I am yours.

[He opens the golden casket.]

Morocco
O hell! what have we here?
A carrion Death, within whose empty eye
There is a written scroll! I'll read the writing.

'All that glisters is not gold,　　　65
Often have you heard that told;
Many a man his life hath sold
But my outside to behold.
Gilded tombs do worms infold.

        Had you been as wise as bold,   70
        Young in limbs, in judgment old,
        Your answer had not been inscroll'd.
        Fare you well, your suit is cold.'

    Cold, indeed, and labour lost,
    Then farewell, heat, and welcome, frost.   75
    Portia, adieu. I have too griev'd a heart
    To take a tedious leave; thus losers part.

[... Later in Act 2, the Prince of Arragon comes to take the caskets challenge.]

Scene 9

[Enter NERISSA, and a Servitor.]

Nerissa

    Quick, quick, I pray thee; draw the curtain straight;
    The Prince of Arragon hath ta'en his oath,
    And comes to his election presently.

[Flourish of Cornets. Enter the PRINCE OF ARRAGON, PORTIA, and their Trains.]

Portia

    Behold, there stand the caskets, noble Prince.
    If you choose that wherein I am contain'd,   5
    Straight shall our nuptial rites be solemniz'd;
    But if you fail, without more speech, my lord,
    You must be gone from hence immediately.

Arragon

    I am **enjoin'd** by oath to observe three things:
    First, never to unfold to any one   10
    Which casket 'twas I chose; next, if I fail
    Of the right casket, never in my life
    To woo a maid in way of marriage;
    Lastly,
    If I do fail in fortune of my choice,   15
    Immediately to leave you and be gone.

Portia

    To these injunctions every one doth swear
    That comes to hazard for my worthless self.

[... He, too, considers the inscriptions.]

[He opens the sliver casket.]

Portia

    [Aside] Too long a pause for that which you find there.

Arragon

    What's here? The portrait of a blinking idiot
    Presenting me a **schedule**! I will read it.   55
    How much unlike art thou to Portia!
    How much unlike my hopes and my deservings!

'Who chooseth me shall have as much as he deserves.'
Did I deserve no more than a fool's head?
Is that my prize? Are my deserts no better? 60

Portia

To offend and judge are distinct offices
And of opposed natures.

Arragon

What is here? *[Reads]*

'**The fire seven times** tried this;
Seven times tried that judgment is
That did never **choose amiss**. 65
Some there be **that shadows kiss**,
Such have but a shadow's bliss.
There be fools alive **iwis**,
Silver'd o'er, and so was this.
Take what wife you will to bed, 70
I will ever be your head.
So be gone; you are sped.'
Still more fool I shall appear
By the time I linger here.
With one fool's head I came to woo, 75
But I go away with two.
Sweet, adieu! I'll keep my oath,
Patiently to bear my wroth.

[Exit with his Train.]

Glossary

A carrion Death: a skull

enjoin'd: bound

schedule: scroll

the fire seven times: silver that has been strengthened seven times in the furnace

choose amiss: choose wrongly

that shadows kiss: chase an illusion or an idea of love

iwis: for sure

silver'd o'er: white or grey haired, in old age

Lesson 8.2.1 — *'All that glisters is not gold'*

Learning objective(s):	**Resources:**
• To explore and interpret the messages on the caskets. • To consider the implications of the casket test.	• PowerPoint 8.2.1 • Extract 8.2.1 • Worksheet 8.2.1

Sensitivity note: This play handles themes of prejudice towards peoples of Jewish faith and culture, and uses the term 'Jew' in a derogatory manner. Please handle these themes sensitively and consider setting ground rules for how your class can discuss this respectfully.

Getting started

- Begin by asking students to recall what they remember from Week 1 about Portia. Where does she live? What do we know about her and her situation? What challenge has been set by her father? Share the lesson objectives with the class on **PowerPoint slide 1** and then distribute **Extract 8.2.1**.
- Share **The story continues …** and then allocate parts for students to read the extracts from Act 2.

Developing skills

- Organise the class into small groups, with half as Team Morocco and half as Team Arragon. Point out that in Shakespearean times 'Arragon' was spelled with two 'r' letters; in modern times this changed to one 'r', as 'Aragon'. Go through **PowerPoint slides 2 and 3** to set prompts for each group of teams to explore the choices and findings of the gold and silver caskets. These slides could be printed for the teams for ease of reference. Allow time for students to work on the possible interpretations of the riddles.
- Take feedback from a range of groups. Suggested responses for Team Morocco might include that:
  - *the inscriptions are presented as thought-provoking riddles*
  - *Morocco finds a skull and a scroll*
  - *his scroll suggests a moral lesson about material wealth and a reminder that material riches mean nothing in death.*

  Team Arragon's responses might include that:
  - *Arragon reminds the audience that he cannot tell others which casket he picked, that he cannot ask for anyone else's hand in marriage if he fails, and that he must leave at once and not speak to Portia if he fails*
  - *he finds a portrait of a fool inside the casket, and a scroll*
  - *the scroll suggests the idea of a foolish man chasing love that isn't real – including the idea of the old fool with silver hair who does not learn from his mistakes.*

- Working with the whole group, display **PowerPoint slide 4** to encourage more depth of thought regarding Portia's situation. Use the prompts on the slide to consider the idea of the caskets challenge as a way of choosing a husband *for* Portia rather than letting her have her own choice. Reflect on the consequences for the suitors of choosing wrongly. What risk do they take? What other character have we witnessed taking a huge risk because of an oath?
- Encourage students to reflect on the stark consequence for Portia of one of the suitors choosing the correct box. What does this mean for her? Consider how she is objectified and relegated to a possession or a prize by the language of this section, for example, '*I am yours*'; '*If you choose that wherein I am contain'd*'. Remind students that in a patriarchal society such as this, once Portia was married, her wealth would immediately become the property of her husband.

Trying it yourself

- Using the template on **Worksheet 8.2.1**, ask students to recreate the scrolls that Morocco and Arragon find in their caskets using modern English. How would their moral lessons read today? Students could add symbols and decorations to the scrolls to illustrate their message.
- You may wish to ask students to prepare for the next lesson by bringing in a selection of their own art and craft materials or prepare a selection of your own.

Worksheet 8.2.1 — 'All that glisters is not gold'

The Prince of Morocco and the Prince of Arragon both failed in the test to win Portia's hand in marriage and were left with a lesson to learn.

Activity

Using the templates below, create your own versions of the riddles that Morocco and Arragon found on the scrolls in their caskets. Rewrite the content of each message in modern English, emphasising the lesson that each man needed to learn. You could add drawings or symbols to illustrate that message.

Lesson 8.2.2

'Who chooseth me shall have as much as he deserves.'

Learning objective(s):	Resources:
• To create a prop design for a casket symbolising the message it contains.	• PowerPoint 8.2.2 • Worksheet 8.2.2 • A range of art and craft materials to create the embellishments for the gold and silver caskets

Sensitivity note: This play handles themes of prejudice towards peoples of Jewish faith and culture, and uses the term 'Jew' in a derogatory manner. Please handle these themes sensitively and consider setting ground rules for how your class can discuss this respectfully.

It is useful to prepare art and craft materials for the worksheet before the lesson, or ask students in advance to bring in materials.

Recap and reflection

- Begin by looking back on the outcomes of the previous lesson. Share some of the students' examples of the rewritten riddles from their scrolls. Share the objective on **PowerPoint slide 1** with the class and explain that this lesson will focus on the caskets themselves. Ensure that students know the word 'properties' in relation to a dramatic production, and that these are usually referred to as 'props'.

- Discuss how a director might choose to use these key props. Will they be visible to the audience? How might different styles of casket or chest be used depending on whether it is a modern or traditional production? One recent production framed the selection of the caskets using the idea of a game show, for example.

Trying it yourself

- Display **PowerPoint slide 2** and outline the task. Distribute **Worksheet 8.2.2** and allow students time to create their design for their casket. Ensure that a range of art and craft materials are available to create the embellishments for the gold and silver caskets. Remind students of the need to include the inscription.

- Aim for students to include the items found in each casket. By a process of elimination, what do students/the audience now realise about the lead casket? Speculate as to why Portia's father might have chosen this casket for her portrait – and thereby her hand in marriage. The completed scrolls and caskets would make an attractive basis for a classroom display of work on the play.

Final task

- Retain the final five to ten minutes of the lesson as a plenary. Display **PowerPoint slide 3** and consider the information the servant brings to Portia (Act 2, Scene 9). What impression is created here of the final suitor? Who might it be? What is ironic about the fact he is bringing 'Gifts of rich value'? How are students feeling about the character of Bassanio at this point?

Worksheet 8.2.2

'Who chooseth me shall have as much as he deserves'

The caskets of gold, silver and lead are some of the key props of this drama. Think about what they might look like, their scale, their inscriptions and their decorations or embellishments.

Activity 1

Choose one of the caskets, gold, silver or lead, to design for a production of *The Merchant of Venice*. Use the template below.

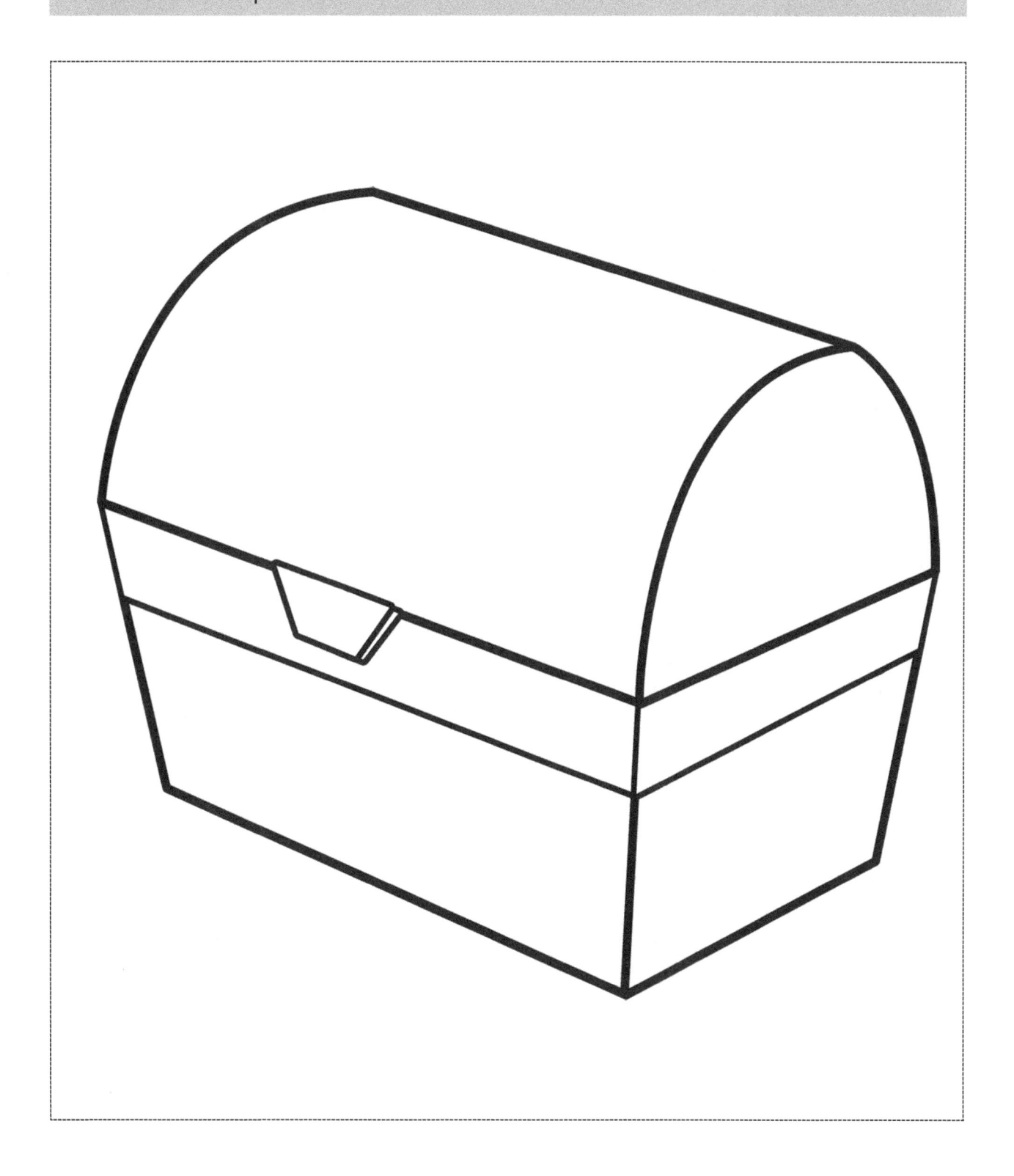

© HarperCollins*Publishers* Ltd 2022

Extract 8.3.1
Act 2 Sc 5
'Look to my house.'

The story continues ...

Back in Venice, Shylock prepares to go and meet with Bassanio. His servant Launcelot warns him that there is a masque or carnival taking place that evening in the streets of Venice. Shylock leaves the keys to the house with his daughter, Jessica, and issues her with a warning.

Shylock

I am bid forth to supper, Jessica;
There are my keys. But wherefore should I go?
I am not bid for love; they flatter me;
But yet I'll go in hate, to feed upon
The **prodigal** Christian. Jessica, my girl,   15
Look to my house. I am right **loath** to go;
There is some ill a-brewing towards my rest,
For I did dream of money-bags to-night.

[... Launcelot tells Shylock of the masque that evening.]

Shylock

What, are there masques? Hear you me, Jessica:
Lock up my doors, and when you hear the drum,
And the vile squealing of the wry-neck'd fife,
Clamber not you up to the **casements** then,   30
Nor thrust your head into the public street
To gaze on Christian fools with varnish'd faces;
But stop my house's ears – I mean my casements;
Let not the sound of shallow **fopp'ry** enter
My sober house. By Jacob's staff, I swear   35
I have no mind of feasting forth to-night;
But I will go. Go you before me, sirrah;
Say I will come.

[...]

[Launcelot exits]

Shylock

[...] Well, Jessica, go in;   50
Perhaps I will return immediately.
Do as I bid you, shut doors after you.
Fast bind, fast find –
A proverb never stale in thrifty mind. *[Exit]*

Glossary

prodigal: reckless and wasteful with money

loath: reluctant

casements: windows

fopp'ry: foolishness

Lesson 8.3.1 — *'Look to my house.'*

Learning objective(s):
- To explore Shylock's use of language.
- To explore the image of the masque and create a contrasting description.

Resources:
- PowerPoint 8.3.1
- Extract 8.3.1
- Worksheet 8.3.1

Sensitivity note: This play handles themes of prejudice towards peoples of Jewish faith and culture, and uses the term 'Jew' in a derogatory manner. Please handle these themes sensitively and consider setting ground rules for how your class can discuss this respectfully.

Getting started

- Distribute **Extract 8.3.1** and share **The story continues ….** Read aloud the first speech from the extract for students or appoint a confident reader. Display **PowerPoint slide 2** and take some initial impressions as to how Shylock seems to be feeling. *Students should pick up on some of the negative language such as 'hate', 'ill a-brewing' and 'loath', using the glossary to help them.*

- Share the lesson objectives on **PowerPoint slide 1** with the class, then read the complete extract.

Developing skills

- Distribute **Worksheet 8.3.1**. Ask students to work in pairs on **Activity 1,** exploring the key aspects of Shylock's language through the speeches. Students may have varied interpretations as the answer to the first question, perhaps relating to the money Shylock is lending to Antonio. Other suggested responses include: *Shylock uses phrases such as 'vile squealing', 'shallow fopp'ry'. There are numerous imperatives such as 'Look to my house', 'Hear you me', 'shut doors'. Students may pick up on how he is anxious, perhaps in a rush. This is reinforced by the questions – his reluctance to go out and his worry about leaving Jessica when there is a masque.* Allow students enough time to explore thoroughly before taking feedback and sharing responses.

- Display **PowerPoint slide 3** showing a painting of a Venetian masque in times gone by. Ask students to consider why Shylock is so concerned about the masque and why he does not want Jessica to witness it or listen to the music. How might this connect with his religious beliefs? Consolidate the impression Shylock paints of the event and how this contrasts with his 'sober house'. How might the painting support Shylock's worries about the masque? *For example, the frivolity, the costumes, the hidden identities/disguises, the elements of flirtation and the seemingly raucous atmosphere.*

- Explain how the Venetian carnival still takes place today and then display **PowerPoint slide 4**. Zoom in to each image in turn, asking students for their impressions of this event and noting these on the board. *Ensure that students pick up on the carnival atmosphere, the boats on the canals and crowds, the flamboyant colours and costumes, the use of disguise and the elaborately painted masks against the backdrop of the beautiful architecture and waterways.*

Trying it yourself

- Ask students to work individually to compete **Activity 2** on the worksheet, carefully considering their own language choices to create a contrasting image of the carnival to Shylock's. For extra challenge, this could be done from the perspective of one of the contrasting characters in the play, for example Lorenzo or Jessica. How might they view this event? Encourage students to use a range of techniques to create the vibrant atmosphere seen in the images.

Taking it further

- To conclude this first lesson, ask students to reflect on the scene and what it shows us about Shylock and how strict he is with his daughter. Display **PowerPoint slide 5** to introduce students to the idea of the patriarchal society. Lead students to make connections between the father and daughter relationship here and what we know of Portia's situation and the limitations placed on her by her father (even from beyond the grave). Take responses from the class. If students have studied *A Midsummer Night's Dream* in Year 7, can they draw on prior learning to connect this with Egeus and Hermia?

Worksheet 8.3.1 — *'Look to my house.'*

In this extract, we learn more about the character of Shylock from the language he uses.

Activity 1

Working with a partner, explore the following aspects of Shylock's language. Record your answers in your notebook.

1. When Shylock mentions his dream, Shakespeare uses foreshadowing, where he hints at possible future events. What might Shylock's dream signify?

2. Make a list of all the phrases Shylock uses to describe the carnival or 'masque'. What impression does he create of this event? How can you tell that he disapproves of it?

3. How many examples can you find of imperatives or command sentences in Shylock's speech? Who is he addressing? What impression does this create of him? What do you imagine his tone of voice would be in delivering this speech? At what kind of pace do you think it would be delivered?

4. Look at Shylock's use of questions in the speech. Does this help us to realise how he is feeling? Does this add to your ideas about the tone he is using and the pace at which he might be speaking?

Activity 2

Think about the picture Shylock has painted for us of the carnival or 'masque'. Using the images on the slides as your inspiration, write a description in your notebook of approximately 250–300 words, painting a contrasting image of a Venetian masque.

You could write this description from the perspective of one of the other characters in the play, such as Lorenzo or even Jessica – perhaps defying her father and looking out at the carnival scene.

Bring to life the colour, costumes and activity, which might include burning torches, boats on the canals, fire eaters, music and performers. Aim to use a range of techniques to create imagery, such as:

- exciting adjectives
- interesting verbs to create movement
- metaphor or simile
- personification
- onomatopoeia.

© HarperCollins*Publishers* Ltd 2022   Year 8, *The Merchant of Venice*, Week 3

Extract 8.3.2 Act 2 Sc 3 — 'Love is blind'

The story continues ...

Shylock's servant Launcelot wants to leave Shylock's employment. He is taken on by Bassanio as his servant, as Bassanio is preparing to travel to Belmont to court Portia. Bassanio's friend Gratiano arrives and asks if he too can accompany him to Belmont.

Launcelot breaks the news to Jessica that he is leaving. Jessica is sad at this news, but she too is planning to leave Shylock's house. We learn that she is in love with Lorenzo, another young Venetian, and he with her. However, the two of them are from different religious faiths, which would prevent them from being together.

Venice. Shylock's house.

[Enter JESSICA and LAUNCELOT.]

Jessica
I am sorry thou wilt leave my father so.
Our house is hell; and thou, a merry devil,
Didst rob it of some taste of tediousness.
But fare thee well; there is a **ducat** for thee;
And, Launcelot, soon at supper shalt thou see   5
Lorenzo, who is thy new master's guest.
Give him this letter; do it secretly.
And so farewell. I would not have my father
See me in talk with thee.

Launcelot
Adieu! tears exhibit my tongue. Most beautiful pagan,   10
most sweet Jew! If a Christian did not play the knave
and get thee, I am much deceived. But, adieu! these
foolish drops do something drown my manly spirit;
adieu!

Jessica
Farewell, good Launcelot. *[Exit]*   15
Alack, what **heinous** sin is it in me
To be asham'd to be my father's child!
But though I am a daughter to his blood,
I am not to his manners. O Lorenzo,
If thou keep promise, I shall end this strife,   20
Become a Christian and thy loving wife.

[Exit]

[... Later that evening when Shylock is meeting with Bassanio, Lorenzo and his friends arrive to help Jessica escape and elope. We move to Scene 6.]

[Enter JESSICA, above, in boy's clothes.]

Jessica

    Who are you? Tell me, for more certainty,
    Albeit I'll swear that I do know your tongue.

Lorenzo

    Lorenzo, and thy love.

Jessica

    Lorenzo, certain; and my love indeed;
    For who love I so much? And now who knows   30
    But you, Lorenzo, whether I am yours?

Lorenzo

    Heaven and thy thoughts are witness that thou art.

Jessica

    Here, catch this casket; it is worth the pains.
    I am glad 'tis night, you do not look on me,
    For I am much asham'd of **my exchange**;   35
    But love is blind, and lovers cannot see
    The pretty follies that themselves commit;
    For, if they could, Cupid himself would blush
    To see me thus transformed to a boy.

Lorenzo

    Descend, for you must be my **torch-bearer**.   40

Jessica

    What! must I hold a candle to my shames?
    They in themselves, good sooth, are too too light.
    Why, 'tis an office of discovery, love,
    And I should be obscur'd.

Lorenzo

                          So are you, sweet,
    Even in the lovely garnish of a boy.   45
    But come at once,
    For the **close night doth play the runaway**,
    And we are stay'd for at Bassanio's feast.

Jessica

    I will make fast the doors, and **gild myself**
    With some more ducats, and be with you straight.   50

                                [Exit above.]

Lorenzo

    Beshrew me, but I love her heartily,
    For she is wise, if I can judge of her,
    And fair she is, if that mine eyes be true,
    And true she is, as she hath prov'd herself;   55
    And therefore, like herself, wise, fair, and true,
    Shall she be placed in my constant soul.

                            [Enter JESSICA, below.]

    What, art thou come? On, gentleman, away!

Glossary

ducat: gold coin

heinous: terrible; monstrous

my exchange: my disguise as a boy

torch-bearer: a young male servant (Jessica is in disguise)

close night doth play the runaway: the time is passing quickly

gild myself: take more gold

Lesson 8.3.2 *'Love is blind'*

Learning objective(s):
- To understand how Shakespeare presents Jessica.
- To consider how Shakespeare creates complex characters.

Resources:
- PowerPoint 8.3.2
- Extract 8.3.2
- Worksheet 8.3.2

Sensitivity note: This play handles themes of prejudice towards peoples of Jewish faith and culture, and uses the term 'Jew' in a derogatory manner. Please handle these themes sensitively and consider setting ground rules for how your class can discuss this respectfully.

Recap and reflection

- Introduce **Extract 8.3.2** by reading **The story continues …**. Share the lesson objectives on **PowerPoint slide 1** with the class. Appoint readers to read aloud the exchanges between Jessica, Launcelot and Lorenzo. Ensure that students know Jessica's plan: draw attention to the letter, the secrecy and the use of the disguise. When does Jessica leave? What had she been entrusted with?
- Display **PowerPoint slide 2**. Refer to the metaphor in the extract describing her home as 'hell'. Reflect on what we know so far about the father and daughter relationship. How strict a father is Shylock? Are there links between Jessica's situation and Portia's? Will Jessica be free to marry Lorenzo, who is from a different faith? Where have we seen conflict between the people of different faiths earlier in the play?

Developing skills

- Ask students to work individually on **Activity 1** on **Worksheet 8.3.2**. The noun phrases include: *most sweet Jew; my father's child; thy loving wife; foolish drops; my manly spirit; heinous sin* and the words used by Lorenzo. Share students' responses to check collaboratively. Then ask students to collect the words Lorenzo uses to describe Jessica at the end of the extract. What do they tell us about his feelings for Jessica and how he perceives her?
- Working with the whole group, display **PowerPoint slide 3** to introduce the idea that Lorenzo uses key adjectives to describe Jessica's qualities. Use the prompt questions on the slide to explore possible comments on the effect of those words.
- Use the prompt questions on **PowerPoint slide 4** to explore how Shakespeare has created complexity in Jessica's character. On the one hand Lorenzo describes her as 'sweet', 'fair', 'wise' and 'true'. Explore the use of those adjectives against the backdrop of what she is doing. Ask students to consider Jessica's actions. Refer students to the interesting verb phrase *'gild myself'*. How does she do this? Is there any justification for her actions? How might her actions lead back to the metaphor in the opening of the extract where she states: *'Our house is hell'*.
- Display **PowerPoint slide 5**. Relate this image of the casket back to students' previous design work and the three caskets that held the key to Portia's future. Jessica also mentions a casket, presumably filled with gold ducats and precious items belonging to her father. Question students about what she does with this casket (for example, she throws it straight to Lorenzo). How might this casket symbolise Jessica's freedom compared with the restrictions Portia's caskets created?
- Display **PowerPoint slide 6**. Ask students to reflect on Jessica's disguise. Why can she not escape as herself? Why is she dressed as a young man? What bold and risky decision does Jessica take into her own hands (for example, *she decides on her own future and her own husband even though it means leaving her home, her father and her faith*). Has love made her 'blind' to this risk?

Final task

- Ask students to work individually on **Activity 2** on the worksheet. Students should create an analytical response exploring Shakespeare's methods in presenting Jessica. Lead them to refer to the use of specific adjectives, noun phrases and the interesting verb phrase, but also to Shakespeare's broader methods, such as the use of the symbolism of the casket and the use of the disguise. Ensure that students follow the method outlined in activity 2.

Taking it further

- Act 2 of this play is lengthy and complex, contrasting the casket scenes in Belmont with the action in Venice. It is advisable to follow this work with a viewing of a production of this whole act. Aim for a recent interpretation that deals sensitively with the complex social issues that Shakespeare brings to light.

Worksheet 8.3.2 — 'Love is blind'

Within the extract we see Jessica described in several ways: by Launcelot, by Lorenzo and by Jessica herself.

Activity 1

Work through the extracts and collect examples of the noun phrases (adjective + noun) that Jessica uses and the ones that Launcelot uses. Write them in the table. An example of each has been given for you.

Noun phrases Jessica uses	Noun phrases Launcelot uses
A merry devil	Most beautiful pagan

Now note down all the words that Lorenzo uses to describe Jessica.

....

....

Activity 2

Complete the response below in your notebook in answer to the question:

How does Shakespeare present the character of Jessica?

In each part of your answer:

- identify a method that Shakespeare uses
- give a precise example or examples
- comment on the effect or impact that choice has on you.

Shakespeare shows us Lorenzo's perception of Jessica by using adjectives such as 'wise', 'fair' and 'true'. This makes us think ...

Shakespeare also uses ...

However, Shakespeare creates a different perception through ...

Extract 8.4.1 Act 3 Sc 1 — 'If you prick us, do we not bleed?'

The story so far ...

Antonio entered into a contract with Shylock to pay back money he borrowed on Bassanio's behalf. In the contract, it states that if Antonio cannot pay back the money, then Shylock will take a pound of flesh from his body. Antonio didn't ever think that such a situation would happen, so freely signed the bond. Unfortunately, Antonio's ships have all been lost at sea, so he now has no means of paying Shylock back, and Shylock, bereft over the loss of Jessica, is determined to get his pound of flesh. Solanio and Salerio have been spreading gossip about the elopement. Their prejudiced views match Antonio's, further antagonising Shylock.

Shylock

[...] He hath disgrac'd me and **hind'red** me half a million; laugh'd at my losses, mock'd at my gains, scorned **my nation**, thwarted my bargains, cooled my friends, heated mine enemies. And what's his reason? I am a Jew. Hath not a Jew eyes? Hath not a Jew hands, organs, **dimensions**, senses, affections, passions, fed with the same food, hurt with the same weapons, subject to the same diseases, healed by the same means, warmed and cooled by the same winter and summer, as a Christian is? If you prick us, do we not bleed? If you tickle us, do we not laugh? If you poison us, do we not die? And if you wrong us, shall we not revenge? If we are like you in the rest, we will resemble you in that. If a Jew wrong a Christian, what is his humility? Revenge. If a Christian wrong a Jew, what should his sufferance be by Christian example? Why, revenge. **The villainy you teach me I will execute; and it shall go hard but I will better the instruction**.

50

55

60

Glossary

Hind'red me: prevented me from making

my nation: a reference to all peoples of the Jewish faith

dimensions: bodily parts

The villainy you teach me I will execute; and it shall go hard but I will better the instruction: I will seek revenge even more strongly than I have been taught.

Lesson 8.4.1 — *'If you prick us, do we not bleed?'*

Learning objective(s):	Resources:
• To understand how to present a viewpoint or perspective, using sound and movement. • To explore opinions through choral speech.	• PowerPoint 8.4.1 • Extract 8.4.1 • Worksheet 8.4.1

Sensitivity note: This play handles themes of prejudice towards peoples of Jewish faith and culture, and uses the term 'Jew' in a derogatory manner. Please handle these themes sensitively and consider setting ground rules for how your class can discuss this respectfully.

Getting started

- Share the lesson objectives on **PowerPoint slide 1** with the class. Then display **PowerPoint slide 2**. Read Extract 8.4.1 to the class. Use the scene and the glossary to consolidate knowledge. Read through the extract twice. Ask students to listen carefully the first time. On the second reading, ask them to list Shylock's arguments for wanting to take revenge. This could be done on whiteboards to be held up at the end. You may wish to pause at each reason, to give students time to write. Shylock's reasons are:
1 Antonio has brought disgrace on Shylock; 2 Antonio has cost him half a million; 3 Antonio laughed when Shylock lost money; 4 Antonio has insulted the Jewish faith and culture; 5 Antonio has prevented Shylock from getting good deals; 6 Because a Jewish person is as human as a Christian person, he will also seek revenge against those who wrong him.

Developing skills

- Display **PowerPoint slide 3**. Explain that a chorus originates in Greek theatre and is a group of actors who speak as one. They are there to comment on or narrate action in the play. Here, we are transforming Shylock's speech into a commentary on one of the key themes of the play. Ask students to work in groups of 4–6 to develop a choral speech that expresses Shylock's thoughts and opinions. Encourage groups to experiment with different ways of saying the lines. For example, each person could say a different line individually, or they might say some lines together, or all the lines in unison. Steer students to consider adding more and more voices as they present the speech, and remind them to focus on which of the words or phrases they will emphasise.

- Stop and check that each group is making progress by listening in to their choral speech. You may want to choose a successful group to demonstrate progress at this point.

- Now ask groups to think of movements or poses to accompany the lines. Encourage creativity. For example, will they all stand in a line? A semi-circle? At different heights? Face different directions? Will they freeze when not speaking? Will they change positions? Add gestures?

- Give groups time to develop their ideas. They should rehearse, putting both speech and movement together.

Trying it yourself

- Display **PowerPoint slide 4** and, in your performance space, get ready to watch each group's work. Choose whether to watch every group or just a few. Remind students that when we watch other people perform, we need to watch and listen carefully without interrupting the performance. When each group is performing, ensure that the audience can see the actions and hear the sounds clearly.

- After each performance, ask for verbal feedback from the class. What ideas did the group capture? Which movements and poses did they use to do this? Is Shylock's speech only about himself or does it paint a bigger picture of how people are treated?

- Display **PowerPoint slide 5** and give students **Worksheet 8.4.1**. Ask them to complete the self-evaluation questions for **After the performance**, where they should reflect on their own participation and the reasons for the choices they made.

Taking it further

- Watch a production or read the whole of Act 3 Scene 1 (pages 96–105 in *Collins Classroom Classics*) to contextualise the extract. Continue by reading Act 3 Scene 2 (pages 106–127).

Worksheet 8.4.1 — 'If you prick us, do we not bleed?'

After the performance

- You have rehearsed and possibly even performed your scene, using choral speech and movement.
- Complete the self-evaluation questions below.

1. What did you think Shylock wanted the listener to know in his speech?

....

....

....

....

....

....

2. Which words or phrases did your group emphasise in the choral speech?

....

....

....

....

....

....

3. How did you emphasise them? (Think about how you said the lines, as well as how you presented ideas through movement.)

....

....

....

....

....

....

Extract 8.4.2
Act 3 Sc 3
'... since I am a dog, beware my fangs'

The story continues ...

Shylock's daughter, Jessica, eloped with Lorenzo and has been staying at Belmont. Meanwhile, after many suitors' attempts at choosing the right casket, Bassanio chooses correctly. Portia is thrilled and they are now able to plan their wedding. As they are celebrating the happy event, news comes of Antonio's predicament. Portia is determined to help her new fiancé's friend by providing money to pay the debt. In this scene, Shylock is determined to win his legal case against Antonio. Antonio, unaware that Bassanio is on his way to help him, accepts his fate, as he respects the rule of law.

Venice. A street.

[Enter SHYLOCK, SOLANIO, ANTONIO, and Gaoler.]

Shylock
Gaoler, **look to him**. Tell not me of mercy –
This is the fool that lent out money **gratis**.
Gaoler, look to him.

Antonio
Hear me yet, good Shylock.

Shylock
I'll have my bond; speak not against my bond.
I have sworn an oath that I will have my bond. 5
Thou call'dst me dog before thou hadst a cause,
But, since I am a dog, beware my fangs;
The Duke shall grant me justice. I do wonder,
Thou **naughty** gaoler, that thou art so fond
To come abroad with him at his request. 10

Antonio
I pray thee hear me speak.

Shylock
I'll have my bond. I will not hear thee speak;
I'll have my bond; and therefore speak no more.
I'll not be made a soft and **dull-ey'd** fool,
To shake the head, relent, and sigh, and yield, 15
To Christian **intercessors**. Follow not;
I'll have no speaking; I will have my bond.

[Exit.]

[...]

Antonio
The Duke cannot deny the course of law;
For the commodity that strangers have

With us in Venice, if it be denied,
Will much impeach the justice of the state,
Since that the trade and profit of the city 30
Consisteth of all nations. Therefore, go;
These griefs and losses have so **bated** me
That I shall hardly spare a pound of flesh
To-morrow to my bloody creditor.
Well, gaoler, on; pray God Bassanio come
To see me pay his debt, and then I care not.

[Exeunt.]

Glossary

look to him: keep a close eye on him

gratis: free from interest

naughty: worth nothing

dull-ey'd: stupid, dim

intercessors: negotiators

bated: physically reduced

Lesson 8.4.2   *'... since I am a dog, beware my fangs'*

Learning objective(s):
- To explore the text through improvisation.
- To investigate writer intention and characterisation.

Resources:
- PowerPoint 8.4.2
- Extract 8.4.2
- Worksheet 8.4.2

Sensitivity note: This play handles themes of prejudice towards peoples of Jewish faith and culture, and uses the term 'Jew' in a derogatory manner. Please handle these themes sensitively and consider setting ground rules for how your class can discuss this respectfully.

Recap and reflection

- Share the lesson objectives on **PowerPoint slide 1** with the class. Then display **PowerPoint slide 2**. Revisit what students remember about the reasons Shylock gives for seeking revenge. This should be done individually and be self-marked. Set a timer for 3 minutes. Whiteboards could be used to record responses. Shylock's reasons are: *1 Antonio has brought disgrace on Shylock; 2 Antonio has cost him half a million; 3 Antonio laughed when Shylock lost money; 4 Antonio has insulted the Jewish faith and culture; 5 Antonio has prevented Shylock from getting good deals; 6 Because a Jewish person is as human as a Christian person, he also will seek revenge against those who wrong him.*

Developing skills

- Hand out **Extract 8.4.2** and display **PowerPoint slide 3**. Ask students to work in pairs to read the extract.
- When they have done this, stop and check their understanding. Discuss the questions on the slide as a class. *Answers: 1 Shylock is determined to have justice/his bond, and for the Gaoler to take Antonio into custody; 2 Accept sensible suggestions, for example: He is fed up with being manipulated. He doesn't believe Antonio has a right to speak; 3 Antonio respects the law. He cannot pay Shylock, so must face the consequences.*
- Ask pairs to improvise an alternative scene, choosing one of the options from the slide: 1. Instead of accepting the rule of law, Antonio argues back; 2. Instead of insisting on revenge, Shylock forgives Antonio.
- Give pairs time to develop their ideas. They should improvise using their own choice of words. Guide students to focus on meaning and characterisation.

Trying it yourself

- Display **PowerPoint slide 4** and, in your performance space, get ready to watch each pair's work. Choose whether to watch every pair or just a few. Remind students that when we watch other people perform, we need to watch and listen carefully without interrupting the performance. When each pair is performing, ensure that the audience can see the actions and hear the sounds clearly.

    After each performance, ask for verbal feedback from the class. Do the alternative scenes alter how we view the characters? Why might Shakespeare have chosen to present Antonio and Shylock in the way he did?

Final task

- Hand out **Worksheet 8.4.2**. Ask students to complete the self-evaluation table by reflecting on their own participation and character choices.

Taking it further

- It would be useful to read on to the end of Act 3 (Scenes 4 and 5, pages 132 to 145) at this point or watch this scene in its entirety. Aim for a recent interpretation that deals sensitively with the complex social issues that Shakespeare brings to light in the play. Pay particular attention to Portia's plan in Act 3 Scene 4 and Jessica's feelings about her father in Act 3 Scene 5.

Worksheet 8.4.2: '... since I am a dog, beware my fangs'

Final task

- You have rehearsed and possibly even performed your improvised alternative scene.
- Complete the self-evaluation table below.

The character I played was:	
How this character was viewed in the original text:	
How I made this character different from the original text:	
Which version I prefer and my reasons why:	

Lesson 8.5.1 *'I crave the law'*

Learning objective(s):	Resources:
• To consolidate understanding of the trial scene. • To consider the key themes of disguise and deception.	• PowerPoint 8.5.1 • Worksheets 8.5.1a–d

Sensitivity note: This play handles themes of prejudice towards peoples of Jewish faith and culture, and uses the term 'Jew' in a derogatory manner. Please handle these themes sensitively and consider setting ground rules for how your class can discuss this respectfully.

Getting started

- Remind students of Portia's secret plan at the end of Act 3. In a brief question and answer, ask students what they can recall of the bond that Antonio signed in Act 1. Can they remember how confident he was? How might he be feeling at this point? What do they feel about the fact that Shylock has asked for a pound of his flesh? Is that feasible? What will happen to Antonio when his flesh is cut?

- Show **PowerPoint slide 1** and share the lesson objectives with the class. Then use **PowerPoint slide 2** to consider the wider implications of Portia's plan. Ensure that students are aware of the use of dramatic irony here, as well as the connection with Jessica – that to exert power and freedom to travel unaccompanied, the women disguise themselves as men. Expand the discussion to think about how the potential, skills and intelligence of women are wasted through inequality. How might this be reflected through other types of inequality or prejudice?

Developing skills

- If students have not undertaken a reciprocal reading lesson of this complete scene at the end of work on Act 3, they should now watch a performance from a film or live production of the play to conceptualise the scene as a whole – perhaps retaining the very end of the scene for the final discussion.

- Organise students into four (or eight) small groups. Distribute the four worksheets (**Worksheets 8.5.1a, b, c, d**) evenly across the groups and display **PowerPoint slide 3**. Each group will be working on a key moment from the trial scene and establishing the key elements of the plot, Portia's arguments and Shylock's responses via the prompt questions on the slide. Allow time for students to discuss and annotate their extracts with their findings.

- Take feedback from the groups, working chronologically through the scene. You may find it useful for students to have copies of the play if you are using editions for reciprocal reading or to have copies of all four worksheets so they can make notes on each other's findings if desired. *Ensure that students are aware of the changing reactions of Shylock; of how Portia focuses on using the precise wording to bring about the 'twist' in the plot.*

- Introduce the key themes we have seen at play in this scene: disguise and deception. Display **PowerPoint slide 4**. Ask students to work in pairs and invite them to make links with earlier events in the play, discussing the prompts and making notes. Take feedback. Students should recall Jessica's disguise, but also lead them to consider other more subtle forms of disguise. Was Bassanio really the man of means he pretended to be to win Portia? Explore the way Portia operates in the trial scene. Is she fair to Shylock? How have the tables been turned on him? Consider how he was also deceived by his daughter when she eloped with Lorenzo.

Trying it yourself

- Consider the ending of this powerful climax to the play. You may wish to watch a performance – or perhaps even two different interpretations – of the very end of Act 4 Scene 1. Using the prompts on **PowerPoint slide 5**, lead students to consider the very real moral dilemma we face as an audience here. Has justice been served and who does it favour? Was Shylock's bond and his demand – essentially for Antonio's life – fair or just? How do students respond to the losses Shylock has suffered: his daughter, his wealth, but also the order that he should change his religion. How do we respond to this as a contemporary audience? Can it be right to ask anyone to change their faith? What if that faith is directly related to their culture?

Worksheet 8.5.1a Act 4 Sc 1
'I crave the law'

Portia, disguised as a lawyer, has just appealed to Shylock to be merciful to Antonio.

Activity

Work with your group to explore the extract using the questions on the slide.

Shylock
My deeds upon my head! I crave the law,
The penalty and forfeit of my bond. 205

Portia
Is he not able to discharge the money?

Bassanio
Yes, here I tender it for him in the court;
Yea, twice the sum; if that will not suffice,
I will be bound to pay it ten times o'er,
On forfeit of my hands, my head, my heart; 210
If this will not suffice, it must appear
That malice bears down truth. And, I beseech you,
Wrest once the law to your authority;
To do a great right do a little wrong,
And curb this cruel devil of his will. 215

Portia
It must not be; there is no power in Venice
Can alter a decree established;
'Twill be recorded for a precedent,
And many an error, by the same example,
Will rush into the state; it cannot be. 220

Shylock
A Daniel come to judgment! Yea, a Daniel!
O wise young judge, how I do honour thee!

Portia
I pray you, let me look upon the bond.

Shylock
Here 'tis, most reverend doctor; here it is.

Portia
Shylock, there's thrice thy money off'red thee. 225

Shylock
An oath, an oath! I have an oath in heaven.
Shall I lay perjury upon my soul?
No, not for Venice.

Worksheet 8.5.1b
Act 4 Sc 1
'I crave the law'

Shylock has rejected Portia's appeal for mercy. Portia, disguised as a lawyer, reads over the bond Antonio signed.

Activity

Work with your group to explore the extract using the questions on the slide.

Portia
>Why, this bond is forfeit;
>And lawfully by this the Jew may claim
>A pound of flesh, to be by him cut off 230
>Nearest the merchant's heart. Be merciful.
>Take thrice thy money; bid me tear the bond.

Shylock
>When it is paid according to the tenor.
>It doth appear you are a worthy judge;
>You know the law; your exposition 235
>Hath been most sound; I charge you by the law,
>Whereof you are a well-deserving pillar,
>Proceed to judgment. By my soul I swear
>There is no power in the tongue of man
>To alter me. I stay here on my bond. 240

Antonio
>Most heartily I do beseech the court
>To give the judgment.

Portia
>Why then, thus it is:
>You must prepare your bosom for his knife.

Shylock
>O noble judge! O excellent young man!

Portia
>For the intent and purpose of the law 245
>Hath full relation to the penalty,
>Which here appeareth due upon the bond.

Shylock
>'Tis very true. O wise and upright judge,
>How much more elder art thou than thy looks!

Worksheet 8.5.1c Act 4 Sc 1
'I crave the law'

Having read the bond Antonio signed, Portia, disguised as a lawyer, states the precise outcome.

Activity

Work with your group to explore the extract using the questions on the slide.

Portia

    A pound of that same merchant's flesh is thine.
    The court awards it and the law doth give it.

Shylock

    Most rightful judge!

Portia

    And you must cut this flesh from off his breast.   300
    The law allows it and the court awards it.

Shylock

    Most learned judge! A sentence! Come, prepare.

Portia

    Tarry a little; there is something else.
    This bond doth give thee here no jot of blood:
    The words expressly are 'a pound of flesh'.   305
    Take then thy bond, take thou thy pound of flesh;
    But, in the cutting it, if thou dost shed
    One drop of Christian blood, thy lands and goods
    Are, by the laws of Venice, confiscate
    Unto the state of Venice.   310

Shylock

    Is that the law?

Portia

    Thyself shalt see the act;
    For, as thou urgest justice, be assur'd
    Thou shalt have justice, more than thou desir'st.

    [...]

Shylock

    I take this offer, then: pay the bond thrice,
    And let the Christian go.

Worksheet 8.5.1d Act 4 Sc 1
'I crave the law'

Using the precise wording of the bond, Portia, disguised as a lawyer, has stated that Shylock may claim his pound of flesh but may not spill one drop of blood to do so. In this way, she saves Antonio's life but points out that Shylock cannot now take the money instead.

Activity

Work with your group to explore the extract using the questions on the slide.

Portia
Thou shalt have nothing but the forfeiture
To be so taken at thy peril, Jew.

Shylock
Why, then the devil give him good of it!
I'll stay no longer question.

Portia
       Tarry, Jew.
The law hath yet another hold on you.   345
It is enacted in the laws of Venice,
If it be prov'd against an alien
That by direct or indirect attempts
He seek the life of any citizen,
The party 'gainst the which he doth contrive   350
Shall seize one half his goods; the other half
Comes to the privy coffer of the state;
And the offender's life lies in the mercy
Of the Duke only, 'gainst all other voice.
In which predicament, I say, thou stand'st;   355
For it appears by manifest proceeding
That indirectly, and directly too,
Thou hast contrived against the very life
Of the defendant; and thou hast incurr'd
The danger formerly by me rehears'd.   360
Down, therefore, and beg mercy of the Duke.

       [...]

Shylock
Nay, take my life and all, pardon not that.   372
You take my house when you do take the prop
That doth sustain my house; you take my life
When you do take the means whereby I live.   375

Portia
What mercy can you render him, Antonio?

[...]

Antonio
    So please my lord the Duke and all the court 378
    To quit the fine for one half of his goods;
    I am content, so he will let me have 380
    The other half in use, to render it
    Upon his death unto the gentleman
    That lately stole his daughter –
    Two things provided more: that, for this favour,
    He presently become a Christian; 385
    The other, that he do record a gift,
    Here in the court, of all he dies possess'd,
    Unto his son Lorenzo and his daughter.

Duke
    He shall do this, or else I do recant
    The pardon that I late pronounced here. 390

Portia
    Art thou contented, Jew? what dost thou say?

Shylock
    I am content.

Lesson 8.5.2 — *'I am arm'd and well prepar'd.'*

Learning objective(s):
- To understand the structure of a five-point narrative.
- To plan and write a narrative based on key ideas from the play.

Resources:
- PowerPoint 8.5.2
- Worksheet 8.5.2

Sensitivity note: This play handles themes of prejudice towards peoples of Jewish faith and culture, and uses the term 'Jew' in a derogatory manner. Please handle these themes sensitively and consider setting ground rules for how your class can discuss this respectfully.

Recap and reflection

- Show **PowerPoint slide 1** and share the lesson objectives with the class. Take a few minutes to reflect on the ideas of disguise and deception from the previous lesson. What do students remember? Who used disguise in Act 4 Scene 1? Do students consider that Portia was deceptive in the way she turned the tables on Shylock? Were they expecting this? Reflect on the way Shakespeare created a suspenseful plot twist in the play through the disguised character of Portia and her arguments, which students explored in their groups.

Developing skills

- Display **PowerPoint slides 2** and **3** and outline the five key elements of a successful narrative: exposition and inciting incident; rising action; climax; falling action and resolution; denouement.
- Distribute **Worksheet 8.5.2** and display **PowerPoint slide 4**. Ask students to work in pairs to recap the plot of the play and annotate the diagram in **Activity 1** with the key events, to consolidate their understanding of the narrative terms. You may wish to revisit slides 2 and 3 as students work, so that they can check explanations and definitions against their choices. They should be able to recall that: *Act 1 establishes the situation with Bassanio and Antonio and the bond with Shylock, as well as introducing Portia and her situation. Act 2 brings the casket scenes and Jessica's elopement with Lorenzo. Act 3 brings the news that Antonio's ships are lost, as well as the scenes of love in Belmont and the departure for Venice/Portia's plan. Act 4 focuses on the trial as the climax of the play.*

Trying it yourself

- Display **PowerPoint slide 5** and introduce the narrative tasks for **Activity 2** on the worksheet. Allow students time to work individually on their plan, guiding their choice of task. Move around the room, checking the plans to guide students into producing a cohesive plot.

Final task

- Recap the parameters on slide 5 before students begin writing, to help them maintain a cohesive structure for their piece of writing and apply prior knowledge of language and imagery for effect. Allow the remainder of the lesson time and potentially homework time for **Activity 3**, the completion of the narrative task based on their plan.

Taking It further

- Follow this up with a reciprocal reading lesson covering the very short Act 4 Scene 2 and the final scene of the play set in Belmont, Act 5 Scene 1 (pages 183 to 207) in *Collins Classroom Classics*.

Worksheet 8.5.2 — 'I am arm'd and well prepar'd.'

Activity 1

Work with a partner and plot the events of the play in sequence on the diagram below up to the end of Act 4.

What do *you* predict will be the ending of the play? Jot your ideas onto the diagram.

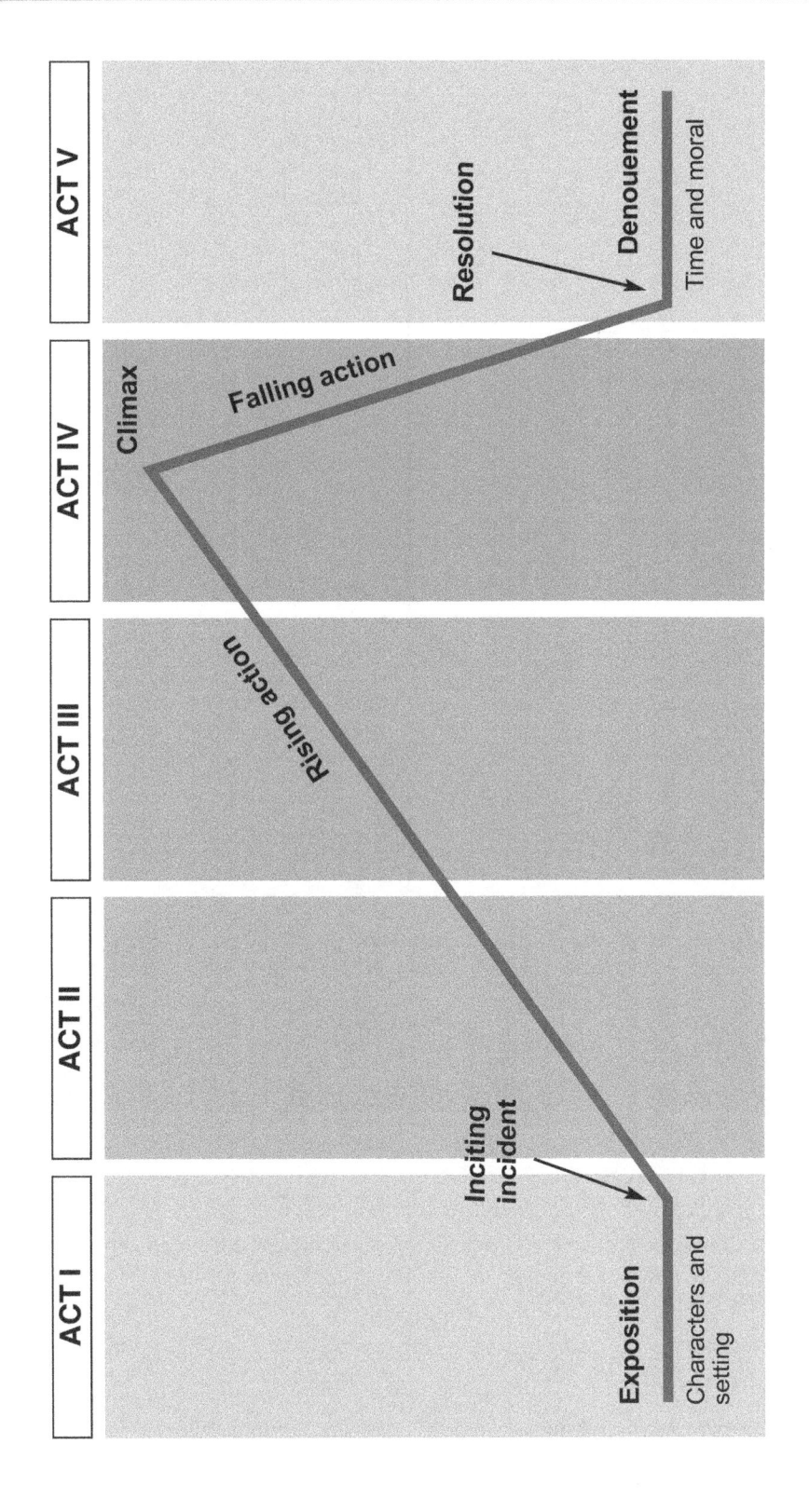

ACT I — Exposition: Characters and setting; Inciting incident

ACT II — Rising action

ACT III — Rising action

ACT IV — Climax; Falling action

ACT V — Resolution; Denouement: Time and moral

Activity 2

You are going to plan and write a story **either** with the title 'Disguised' **or** a story that is based around a moral dilemma.

Use the narrative 'mountain' below to plan the structure and plot of your story.

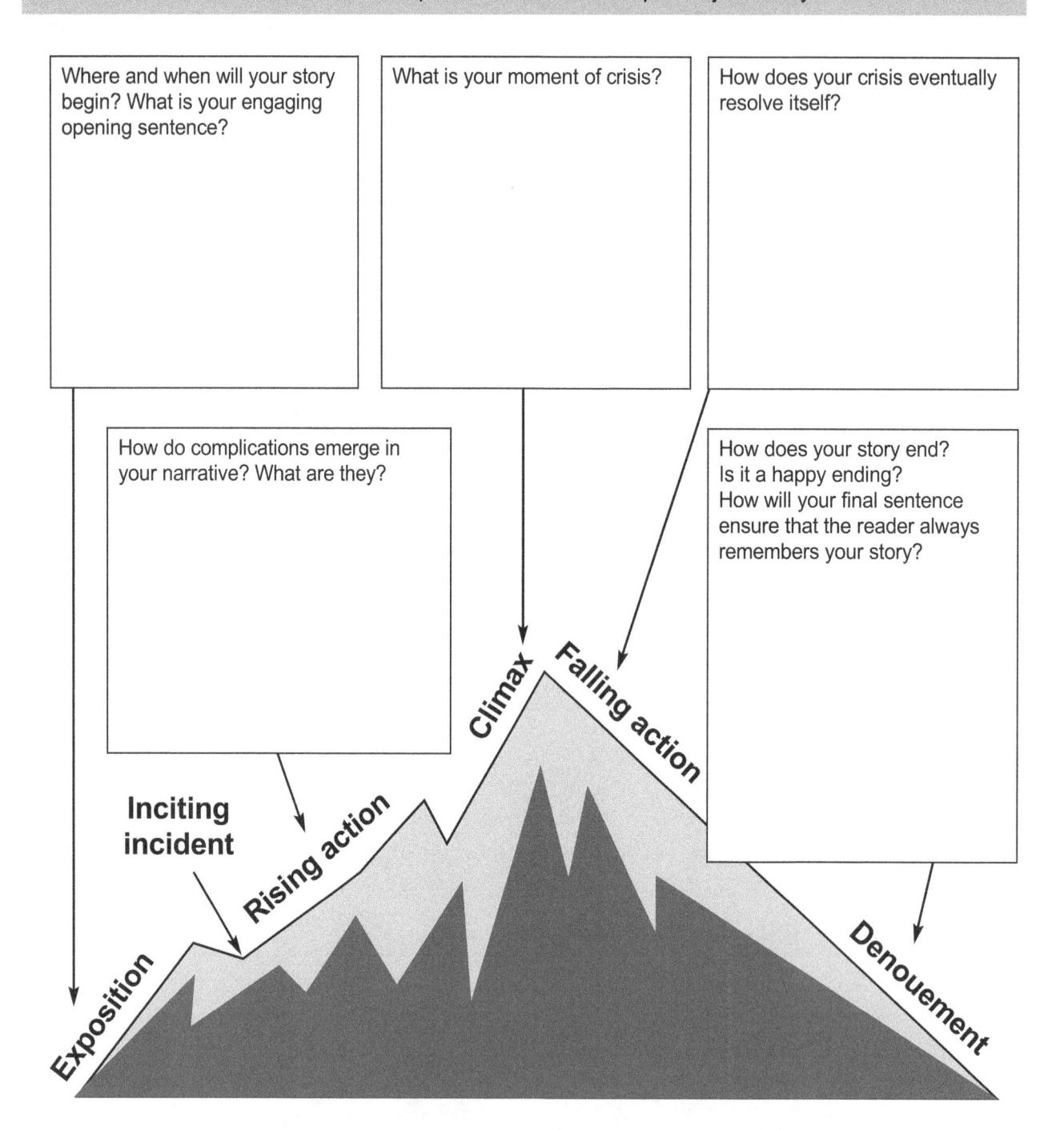

- Where and when will your story begin? What is your engaging opening sentence?
- What is your moment of crisis?
- How does your crisis eventually resolve itself?
- How do complications emerge in your narrative? What are they?
- How does your story end? Is it a happy ending? How will your final sentence ensure that the reader always remembers your story?

Exposition → **Inciting incident** → **Rising action** → **Climax** → **Falling action** → **Denouement**

Activity 3

You are now going to write up your narrative using the structure in your plan. Remember to:

- follow the sequence in your plan
- use exciting vocabulary
- aim to use language features such as similes to create imagery
- check your accuracy carefully as you work.

Extract 8.6.1
Act 4 Sc 1 — 'The quality of mercy is not strain'd'

The story concludes ...

While still in disguise, Portia and Nerissa ask for the rings worn by Bassanio and Gratiano as a payment for the help they have given Antonio. Bassanio and Gratiano agree very reluctantly as the rings were given to them by their new wives. Back in Belmont, Jessica and Lorenzo have remained at Portia's house. Portia and Nerissa arrive back in Belmont before their husbands. They play a joke on their new husbands by asking to see the rings they had gifted them. The scene ends happily with the news that some of Antonio's ships have returned safely after he had feared that they were lost. Shylock, however, is absent from this final act. We learn that his wealth will be inherited by Lorenzo.

Portia

> The quality of mercy is not **strain'd**;
> It droppeth as the gentle rain from heaven
> Upon the place beneath. It is twice blest:
> It blesseth him that gives and him that takes.   185
> 'Tis mightiest in the mightiest; it **becomes**
> The throned monarch better than his crown;
> His sceptre shows the force of temporal power,
> The attribute to awe and majesty,
> Wherein doth sit the dread and fear of kings;   190
> But **mercy is above this sceptred sway**,
> It is enthroned in the hearts of kings,
> It is an attribute to God himself;
> And earthly power doth then show likest God's
> When mercy **seasons** justice. Therefore, Jew,   195
> Though justice be thy plea, consider this –
> That in the course of justice none of us
> Should see salvation; we do pray for mercy,
> And that same prayer doth teach us all to render
> The deeds of mercy. I have spoke thus much   200
> To mitigate the justice of thy plea,
> Which if thou follow, this strict court of Venice
> Must needs give sentence 'gainst the merchant there.

Glossary

strain'd: constrained, restricted or limited

becomes: suits

mercy is above this sceptred sway: being merciful is greater than the power of a king

seasons: is part of

Lesson 8.6.1 — 'The quality of mercy is not strain'd'

Learning objective(s):
- To explore key themes and ideas in the play.
- To reflect on the treatment of Shylock.

Resources:
- PowerPoint 8.6.1
- Extract 8.6.1
- Worksheet 8.6.1

Sensitivity note: This play handles themes of prejudice towards peoples of Jewish faith and culture, and uses the term 'Jew' in a derogatory manner. Please handle these themes sensitively and consider setting ground rules for how your class can discuss this respectfully.

Getting started

- Show **PowerPoint slide 1** and share the lesson objectives with the class. Then display **PowerPoint slide 2**. Ask students to think back over the play, reminding them how it asks us to deal with some very important and sensitive issues. Ask students to work in pairs to consider where we have seen evidence of the themes listed in the bullet points and make notes of their recollections in their notebook. Invite students to share their responses and add to their notes. Suggested responses might include: *the initial exposition of the abuse Shylock had received; Portia's attitudes to her suitors; Shylock's desire for revenge on Antonio; Antonio forgiving Bassanio for losing his money; the justice of Portia finding the husband she wanted; the injustice of the bond and the trial; the double standards applied to citizens of Venice from different religions and cultures; the gender double standards throughout the play.*

Developing skills

- Distribute **Extract 8.6.1** and **Worksheet 8.6.1** and read aloud **The story concludes …**; then read aloud Portia's speech from Act 4 Scene 1 or appoint a confident reader. Decide together on a definition of what 'mercy' is and write this on the board. Consolidate what it means and what we understand by this abstract noun. Still working in pairs for support, ask students to complete **Activity 1**, exploring Portia's speech in more detail. Answers include: *1 'It droppeth as the gentle rain from heaven'; 2 It blesses those who are merciful to others and those who receive the mercy; 3 She shows it as being more powerful than kingship and suggests that its origins lie with God; 4 She asks Shylock to show mercy to Antonio; 5 She addresses Shylock disrespectfully as 'Jew' and not by his name.*

- Lead on from the final question by asking students how they feel about this. Why does Portia not use Shylock's name? What does this tell us about how she sees him? Display **PowerPoint slide 3** and ask students to form small discussion groups. Allow some time for students to reflect on the statement. Allow some time for feeding back student responses and thoughts.

- Display **PowerPoint slide 4** and introduce students to the dramatic device of soliloquy. Reflect on the painting on the slide, which shows Shylock leaving the Duke's palace after the court scene. Take suggestions as to what Shylock might have been thinking and feeling at this point. Does he seem angry and vengeful here, or much more vulnerable? Might he be thinking of his daughter, Jessica, and how he has lost her or is he thinking of his lost wealth? Might he be reflecting on his decision to make the bond with Antonio in the first place?

Trying it yourself

- Using **Activity 2** on the worksheet, set the task for writing a final soliloquy for Shylock in your notebook. Students should do this in modern English to work on the clarity of their ideas, unless they are very confident and would like to aim for presenting their work in verse or even 'in the style of' Shakespeare.

Worksheet 8.6.1: 'The quality of mercy is not strain'd'

Activity 1

Working with a partner, discuss the following questions and then answer them on the lines provided or in your notebook.

1. What simile does Portia use to describe mercy?

   ....

2. Why does Portia describe mercy as being 'twice blest'? In what way does it bring two lots of blessing?

   ....

3. How does Portia show the importance of mercy? What religious reference does she use to add weight to her argument?

   ....

   ....

4. What is she asking Shylock to do in this speech?

   ....

   ....

5. Even though Portia is asking Shylock to be kind and merciful here, what do you notice about how she addresses Shylock?

   ....

   ....

Activity 2

Imagine that you are working on a new production of *The Merchant of Venice*. The director has decided to include a final scene in Act 5 with Shylock alone on the stage.

Write a final speech or soliloquy for Shylock, exploring his thoughts and feelings at the end of the play. Aim to include:

- his reactions to the events in Venice and the courtroom
- how he feels he has been treated
- his thoughts on the losses he has suffered
- whether he has any regrets or would choose to do anything differently.

Lesson 8.6.2 — 'Still have I borne it with a patient shrug'

Learning objective(s):	Resources:
• To explore the wider issues and intentions of the play in a modern context.	• PowerPoint 8.6.2 • Worksheet 8.6.2 • Large sheets of paper and marker pens

Sensitivity note: This play handles themes of prejudice towards peoples of Jewish faith and culture, and uses the term 'Jew' in a derogatory manner. Please handle these themes sensitively and consider setting ground rules for how your class can discuss this respectfully.

Recap and reflection

- Show **PowerPoint slide 1** and share the lesson objectives with the class. Display **PowerPoint slide 2** and use the prompt questions to stimulate initial thoughts from students. Use the proverb to reflect on some of the key issues of the play. What actions prompted Shylock to feel so much hatred for Antonio? Lead into a discussion about the power of hurtful words and how they can impact and stay with someone, affecting and hurting their feelings.

- Explore this more deeply using **PowerPoint slide 3**. Aim to show how Shakespeare's key themes in the play are still just as relevant today and that is why we study his writing and find much to learn from his characters.

Developing skills

- Organise students into small groups and share the group task on **PowerPoint slide 4**. Spend some time unpacking the task, using **Worksheet 8.6.2** as support and explaining what a podcast is for those who are unfamiliar with the term. Some students may be listeners of current (at time of publication) podcasts such as: Stuff You Missed in History Class; The Breakfast Club with DJ Envy; My Favorite Murder; TED Talks; What's Good Games; Socially Awkward or Teen Girl Talk. You could allow 10–15 minutes to listen to an example that you have chosen, which is suitable for your setting.

- Allow time for students to work in their groups, generating initial ideas around the title of the podcast on large sheets of paper with marker pens. Prompt students, for example, to think about the impact of commenting on someone else's appearance, as well as the more serious aspects of prejudice; invite them to consider that what some might consider harmless banter can be hurtful to others, especially if it comes from someone in a majority culture, against someone in a minoritised culture. Encourage them to relate their podcast to issues or attitudes they might like to see changed or challenged within school.

Trying it yourself

- Encourage students to then shape those ideas and consider how they will present them. Will they use a host and guest format, or a more collaborative and shared approach? It is useful to ask students to consider timing, structure and sequence at this stage.

- Move students into writing and producing their content. This could be done individually or collaboratively, depending on the group.

Final task

- Allow some rehearsal time for students to piece together their group outcomes.

- If time allows, this could stretch over two lessons to allow for the content and rehearsal to be perfected. If facilities allow, the podcasts could be recorded and perhaps even used and celebrated in school.

Worksheet 8.6.2: 'Still have I borne it with a patient shrug'

A podcast is a spoken-word programme – like a radio show – that can be downloaded and listened to digitally. It often features a host in discussion with others about a particular topic or issue.

Activity

Working in a small group, you are going to create and write a podcast called:

'Sticks and stones may break my bones, but words will never hurt me.'

Create and write a five-minute podcast to help young people think about and understand the importance of treating each other with respect and seeing our individuality and differences as valuable and something to celebrate, rather than as something to criticise and make fun of.

You could:

- Appoint a host for your podcast to ask the questions.
- Allocate roles for yourselves as a series of guests, or speak and present in turn, sharing your points of view.

You will need to:

- Plan any questions that will be raised in your podcast and draft your answers.
- Ensure that you raise a range of interesting points of view.
- Create a sequence for your programme and consider how you will introduce it and how you will end it.

You should think about:

- What the main issues are related to prejudice and discrimination in relation to young people.
- How young people might be affected by the words and actions of others.
- How we can work together to solve those issues and educate others.
- Key advice and help for anyone who has faced prejudice, unfair treatment or discrimination.

Extract 9.1.1 Act 1 Sc 1 — *'Rebellious subjects, enemies to peace'*

The story so far …

A bitter feud has long been fought between two wealthy and influential households in Verona: the Capulets and the Montagues. This feud has become increasingly violent and has disturbed the peace of the streets. Two young men from the Capulet household are out in the streets, showing off about what they would do to the Montague men and women if they were to meet them. They see more young men from the Montague household and provoke them. This leads to an intense fight. Benvolio, from the Montague household, tries to break it up but comes face to face with an angry Tybalt, a Capulet.

Benvolio

Part, fools! *[Beats down their swords]*
Put up your swords; you know not what you do.

[Enter TYBALT.]

Tybalt

What, art thou drawn among these **heartless hinds**? 60
Turn thee, Benvolio; look upon thy death.

Benvolio

I do but keep the peace; put up thy sword,
Or manage it to part these men with me.

Tybalt

What, drawn, and talk of peace! I hate the word,
As I hate hell, all Montagues, and thee. 65
Have at thee, coward!

[They fight.]

[Enter an officer, and three or four citizens with clubs or partisans.]

[…]

[Enter OLD CAPULET in his gown, and his WIFE]

Capulet

What noise is this? Give me my long sword, ho!

Lady Capulet

A crutch, a crutch! Why call you for a sword? 70

Capulet

My sword, I say! Old Montague is come,
And flourishes his blade in spite of me.

[Enter OLD MONTAGUE and his WIFE.]

Montague

Thou villain Capulet! – Hold me not, let me go.

Lady Montague
> Thou shalt not stir a foot to seek a foe.

[Enter PRINCE ESCALUS with his TRAIN.]

Prince
> Rebellious subjects, enemies to peace, 75
> **Profaners** of this neighbour-stained steel –
> Will they not hear? What, ho! you men, you beasts,
> That quench the fire of your **pernicious** rage
> With purple fountains issuing from your veins!
> On pain of torture, from those bloody hands 80
> Throw your mistempered weapons to the ground,
> And hear the sentence of your moved prince.
> Three civil brawls, bred of an airy word,
> By thee, old Capulet, and Montague,
> Have thrice disturbed the quiet of our streets 85
> And made Verona's ancient citizens
> Cast by their **grave beseeming ornaments**
> To wield **old partisans**, in hands as old,
> **Canker'd** with peace, to part your canker'd hate.
> If ever you disturb our streets again, 90
> Your lives shall pay the forfeit of the peace.
> For this time all the rest depart away.
> You, Capulet, shall go along with me;
> And, Montague, come you this afternoon,
> To know our farther pleasure in this case, 95
> To old Free-town, our common judgment-place.
> Once more, on pain of death, all men depart.

Glossary

heartless hinds: cowardly timid creatures (a hind is a female deer)

profaners: abusers

pernicious: wicked

grave beseeming ornaments: civilised behaviours

old partisans: old grudges

canker'd: diseased

Lesson 9.1.1 — 'Rebellious subjects, enemies to peace'

Learning objective(s):
- To understand the conflict between the Montagues and Capulets.
- To introduce the character of Romeo.

Resources:
- PowerPoint 9.1.1
- Extract 9.1.1
- Worksheet 9.1.1

Getting started

- Distribute **Extract 9.1.1** and read **The story so far …** aloud, then allocate parts to some confident readers. With a less confident group, you may wish to take the role of the Prince to model reading with expression to aid understanding. Share the lesson objectives on **PowerPoint slide 1** with the class and then display **PowerPoint slide 2**. Working with the whole class, use the prompt questions to explore the contrast between the actions and dialogue of Benvolio and Tybalt. Take suggestions of initial impressions and inferences, bringing out the fact that Benvolio is aiming to halt the conflict, while Tybalt is more aggressive and threatening.

Developing skills

- Using the ideas from the whole-class discussion, ask students to work individually to write a paragraph to consolidate those ideas using the clear comprehension method outlined on **PowerPoint slide 3**.

- Distribute **Worksheet 9.1.1** and ask students to work in small groups on **Activity 1**. Students should look again at the Prince's proclamation. They could use three colours of highlighter pens and pencils to complete the first part of the activity, identifying and retrieving the information the Prince gives us about the history of the feud and how it has affected the citizens of Verona, the severe consequences of more disturbances, and key words or phrases that show his displeasure. Students should then move on from the retrieval aspect to consider the possible implications and make some predictions. Allow time for a brief plenary discussion here to check ideas and suggestions.

- Remind students that at this point in the plot, we have yet to meet either of the main characters. Take a moment to explore why students think Shakespeare chose to begin his play in such a violent and aggressive way. Then introduce the idea of contrast and juxtaposition and re-read **The story so far …** on **Extract 9.1.1** to contextualise the next activity.

- Explain that after the prince's decree, Lord and Lady Montague confide in Benvolio that they are worried about their son, Romeo, and ask for his help. Then display **PowerPoint slide 4** and ask students to consider the four quotations. Ask students to work in pairs to think about and discuss why Romeo's parents are worried. What is suggested about his behaviour? Where has he been seen? In feedback, ask students what impression we have of Romeo's character even before we meet him. Does he seem to have more in common with Benvolio or with Tybalt?

- Retaining the same pairs, ask students to read the next section of Act 1 Scene 1 from their worksheet, reading aloud, taking one role each. Students should then explore this section using **Activity 2**, making notes on the four prompt questions on the worksheet, which guide them through the content. Check understanding in a brief plenary. Students should have picked up on: *Romeo is sad because he is in love but not loved in return; he is feeling that love is problematic, painful and chaotic; that his loved one has vowed not to marry or love anyone and asked Romeo to forget her; Benvolio advises Romeo to look for someone else who is just as beautiful.*

Trying it yourself

- Now ask students to work individually to complete the longer comprehension task, **Activity 3** on the worksheet, consolidating their knowledge from the paired exploration. Remind students of the clear method before they begin.

Taking it further

- It is useful at this point for students to watch the opening of the play on a film or streamed production to conceptualise the whole of this opening scene and be able to recognise the contrasts and oppositions Shakespeare has set up. If time allows, read the Prologue on page 3 of *Collins Classroom Classics* and discuss with students if their earlier predictions are similar to or different from the information that the Prologue supplies.

Worksheet 9.1.1 — 'Rebellious subjects, enemies to peace'

Activity 1

Re-read the Prince's speech from your extract where he gives both families a serious warning. Use three different colours to identify and annotate:

- what the Prince says has happened in the past
- what the Prince says must happen in the future
- six key words or phrases that show how the Prince feels about the Capulet–Montague feud.

Work in small groups to discuss and make notes about the following:

- What are the consequences of this fight, according to the Prince?
- How does this set up dramatic tension for the future?
- What do you predict will happen next?

Activity 2

Read the following extract from Act 1 Scene 1, in which Benvolio attempts to find out what is troubling his friend, making notes to identify:

- What is the cause of Romeo's sadness?
- How is he feeling about love?
- What has his loved one sworn to do and why is this a problem for Romeo?
- What does Benvolio suggest as the best solution?

Benvolio   […] What sadness lengthens Romeo's hours?

Romeo   Not having that which having makes them short.

Benvolio   In love?

Romeo   Out –   160

Benvolio   Of love?

Romeo   Out of her favour where I am in love.

Benvolio   Alas that love, so gentle in his view,
Should be so tyrannous and rough in proof!

Romeo   Alas that love, whose view is muffled still,   165
Should without eyes see pathways to his will!
Where shall we dine? O me! What fray was here?

Yet tell me not, for I have heard it all.
Here's much to do with hate, but more with love.
Why then, O brawling love! O loving hate! 170
O anything, of nothing first create!
O heavy lightness! serious vanity!
Mis-shapen chaos of well-seeming forms!
Feather of lead, bright smoke, cold fire, sick health!
Still-waking sleep, that is not what it is! 175
This love feel I, that feel no love in this.
Dost thou not laugh?

Benvolio

No, coz, I rather weep.

Romeo

Good heart, at what?

Benvolio

At thy good heart's oppression.

[...]

Romeo

Well, in that hit you miss: she'll not be hit
With Cupid's arrow. She hath Dian's wit;
And in strong proof of chastity well arm'd,
From Love's weak childish bow she lives unharm'd. 205
She will not stay the siege of loving terms,
Nor bide th' encounter of assailing eyes,
Nor ope her lap to saint-seducing gold.
O, she is rich in beauty; only poor
That, when she dies, with beauty dies her store. 210

Benvolio

Then she hath sworn that she will still live chaste?

Romeo

She hath, and in that sparing makes huge waste;
For beauty, starv'd with her severity,
Cuts beauty off from all posterity.
She is too fair, too wise, wisely too fair, 215
To merit bliss by making me despair:
She hath forsworn to love, and in that vow
Do I live dead that live to tell it now.

Benvolio

Be rul'd by me: forget to think of her.

Romeo

O, teach me how I should forget to think! 220

Benvolio

By giving liberty unto thine eyes.
Examine other beauties.

Activity 3

Write a paragraph, answering the following question.

What have you learned about the character of Romeo so far – from what he has told us and from what other characters have told us?

In your answer, remember to:

- use clear statement sentences
- use supporting quotations from the play to back up your statements
- make inferences to show the depth of your understanding.

Extract 9.1.2 Act 1 Sc 2; Sc 3

'How stands your disposition to be married?'

The story continues ...

After the Prince's decree, Lord and Lady Montague confide in Benvolio that they are worried about their son Romeo and ask for his help.

While Romeo mourns the loss of his love Rosaline, another young man has thoughts of love. The County Paris visits Lord Capulet to ask for his daughter's hand in marriage. His daughter is Juliet.

Extract 1, Act 1 Scene 2

[*Enter* CAPULET, COUNTY PARIS, *and the* CLOWN, *his servant.*]

Capulet
But Montague is bound as well as I,
In penalty alike; and 'tis not hard, I think,
For men so old as we to keep the peace.

Paris
Of honourable reckoning are you both,
And pity 'tis you liv'd at odds so long. 5
But now, my lord, what say you to my **suit**?

Capulet
But saying o'er what I have said before:
My child is yet a stranger in the world,
She hath not seen the change of fourteen years;
Let two more summers wither in their pride 10
Ere we may think her ripe to be a bride.

Paris
Younger than she are happy mothers made.

Capulet
And too soon **marr'd** are those so early made.
The earth hath swallowed all my hopes but she;
She is the hopeful lady of my earth. 15
But woo her, gentle Paris, get her heart;
My will to her consent is but a part.
And, she agreed, within her scope of choice
Lies my consent and fair according voice.
This night I hold an old accustom'd feast, 20
Whereto I have invited many a guest,
Such as I love; and you among the store,
One more, most welcome, makes my number more.
At my poor house look to behold this night
Earth-treading stars that make dark heaven light. 25
Such comfort as do lusty young men feel
When well-apparell'd April on the heel
Of limping winter treads, even such delight

	Among fresh female buds shall you this night	
	Inherit at my house. Hear all, all see,	30
	And like her most whose merit most shall be;	
	Which on more view of many, mine, being one,	
	May stand in number, though in reck'ning none.	
	Come, go with me. *[To* SERVANT, *giving him a paper]*	
	Go, sirrah, trudge about	
	Through fair Verona; find those persons out	35
	Whose names are written there, and to them say	
	My house and welcome on their pleasure stay.	

Extract 2, Act 1 Scene 3

Meanwhile, Lady Capulet tells Juliet of Paris's visit to her father.

Lady Capulet		
	Marry, that 'marry' is the very theme	
	I came to talk of. Tell me, daughter Juliet,	65
	How stands your disposition to be married?	
Juliet		
	It is an honour that I dream not of.	
Nurse		
	An honour! Were not I thine only nurse,	
	I would say thou hadst suck'd wisdom from thy teat.	
Lady Capulet		
	Well, think of marriage now. Younger than you,	70
	Here in Verona, **ladies of esteem**,	
	Are made already mothers. By my count,	
	I was your mother much upon these years	
	That you are now a maid. Thus, then, in brief:	
	The valiant Paris seeks you for his love.	75
Nurse		
	A man, young lady! lady, such a man	
	As all the world – why, he's **a man of wax**.	
Lady Capulet		
	Verona's summer hath not such a flower.	
Nurse		
	Nay, he's a flower; in faith, a very flower.	
Lady Capulet		
	What say you? Can you love the gentleman?	80
	This night you shall behold him at our feast;	
	Read o'er the volume of young Paris' face,	
	And find delight writ there with beauty's pen;	
	Examine every **married lineament**,	
	And see how one another lends content;	85
	And what obscur'd in this fair volume lies	
	Find written in the margent of his eyes.	
	This precious book of love, this unbound lover,	
	To beautify him, only lacks a cover.	
	The fish lives in the sea, and 'tis much pride	90

	For fair without the fair within to hide:	
	That book in many's eyes doth share the glory	
	That in gold clasps locks in the golden story;	
	So shall you share all that he doth possess,	
	By having him making yourself no less.	95

Nurse

No less! Nay, bigger; women grow by men.

Lady Capulet

Speak briefly, can you like of Paris' love?

Juliet

I'll look to like, if looking liking move;
But **no more deep will I endart mine eye**
Than your consent gives strength to make it fly.   100

Glossary

suit: request to marry Juliet

marr'd: ruined

earth-treading stars: beautiful girls

ladies of esteem: young ladies of wealth and status

a man of wax: a perfect model of a man

married lineament: feature of his face

no more deep will I endart mine eye: I won't look any further; anywhere else

Lesson 9.1.2 — *'How stands your disposition to be married?'*

Learning objective(s):	Resources:
• To introduce the theme of love and marriage. • To understand how Shakespeare presents different attitudes to love and marriage based on gender.	• PowerPoint 9.1.2 • Extract 9.1.2 • Worksheet 9.1.2a; 9.1.2b

Recap and reflection

- Ask students to recall what they know about Romeo and share some of their observations from their final piece of work in the last lesson. Hand out **Extract 9.1.2** and read aloud **The Story continues ...** to recap the previous lesson and introduce the main topic of this lesson. Share the lesson objectives with the class on **PowerPoint slide 1**.

- Display **PowerPoint slide 2** and ask students to consider the two quotations that come from the scenes to be studied in this lesson. What do they imply? Who might have said each one: Juliet's mother or father? Ask students to consider the image on the slide and take their first impressions and observations. Consider if anyone looks happy; in love; celebratory. Could this be a poor family wedding or that of a wealthy family? What do they notice about the possible ages of the bride and groom? How do we respond to this from a contemporary perspective?

Developing skills

- Display **PowerPoint slide 3**. Divide the class into small groups with half of the groups labelled Team Paris and half labelled Team Juliet. Distribute the worksheets to the respective teams: **Worksheet 9.1.2a** to the Teams Paris and **Worksheet 9.1.2b** to the Teams Juliet. Allow time for the teams to practise and polish their reading of the extracts using the advice on the worksheet (**Activity 1**), and for them to consider their four exploratory questions and prepare their findings to present back (**Activity 2**).

- Invite groups to present their readings and the findings from both sets of teams, which should include: *Team Paris: Paris is asking for Juliet's hand in marriage; he has to seek permission from her father in this patriarchal society; Lord Capulet feels she is still too young and is worried because she is his only remaining child – marriage would lead to childbirth, which could be fatal; Capulet suggests that Paris should attend their feast that night, which will allow Juliet to make his acquaintance and see if she would consent to the match; Capulet seems genuinely caring and concerned for his daughter's wellbeing at this point. Team Juliet: Lady Capulet is abrupt and direct with Juliet as if this were a simple question and not one that would affect her future life; she reveals that she was married at a similar age to Juliet and was her mother soon after; she does not seem close or compassionate or want a different life for her daughter; Lady Capulet presents Paris as a book to be studied and read and focuses on his appearance and wealth; she seems to feel marriage is simply about extending wealth and influence and suggests that this will elevate Juliet's status; the news seems to come as a shock/surprise to Juliet, though she is polite to her mother 'an honour I dream not of'.*

- Display **PowerPoint slide 4**. Ask: How might these factors help us to understand more about the painting on **slide 2**? How might they help us to understand Juliet's situation at this point in the play? Do they surprise us in any way?

Final task

- Show **PowerPoint slide 5** and allow students some time to work in pairs to consider the statement in light of their earlier explorations, acquired knowledge and the key factors on **slide 4**. Ask them to consider the contrasting views of the parents. Would they have expected Lord Capulet to be more in favour of the early marriage and Lady Capulet more in favour of waiting? Why is it surprising that they take an opposing view? What might be their reasoning?

Worksheet 9.1.2a

'How stands your disposition to be married?'

Team Paris

Activity 1

Allocate parts in your group and practise reading **Extract 1, Act 1 Scene 2** together.

- Remember to read by sentence and not by line.
- Remember to think carefully about the tone and meaning behind the words, and the mood/attitude of the characters in the exchanges you read.
- Remember that 95% of the words used by Shakespeare are still in use today – only some of the phrases and idioms are unfamiliar because Shakespeare lived and wrote 400 years ago. He used different slang words, swear words and cultural references. He might find it difficult to understand some of ours today, so don't let that stand in your way.
- Think about how you will present this scene to the class to bring out its key ideas. What do you really need to emphasise and make clear? Do you want to use a narrator?

Activity 2

Explore these key questions together. You are going to present your findings to the class to share your expert knowledge of the scene. Where you can, use and include the text as evidence for your ideas when you share them with the rest of the class. Make some notes below before presenting your findings.

1. Why has the County Paris come to visit Lord Capulet? What is his intention? Why is he speaking to Juliet's father and not to Juliet herself? Do you think he has even met her at this point? Why? Why not?
2. Lord Capulet seems reluctant to agree to an early marriage. What reasons does he give for this? What does he say has happened to all his other children?
3. What suggestion does Lord Capulet make to Paris and what does he invite him to do?
4. At this point in the play, what kind of a father does Lord Capulet seem to be? What is he allowing his daughter to do and why might this seem unusual?

....

....

....

....

....

....

Worksheet 9.1.2b

'How stands your disposition to be married?'

Team Juliet

Activity 1

Allocate parts in your group and practise reading **Extract 2, Act 1 Scene 3** together.

- Remember to read by sentence and not by line.
- Remember to think carefully about the tone and meaning behind the words, and the mood/attitude of the characters in the exchanges you read.
- Remember that 95% of the words used by Shakespeare are still in use today – only some of the phrases and idioms are unfamiliar because Shakespeare lived and wrote 400 years ago. He used different slang words, swear words and cultural references. He might find it difficult to understand some of ours today, so don't let that stand in your way.
- Think about how you will present this scene to the class to bring out its key ideas. What do you really need to emphasise and make clear? Do you want to use a narrator?

Activity 2

Explore these key questions together. You are going to present your findings to the class to share your expert knowledge of the scene. Where you can, use and include the text as evidence for your ideas when you share them with the rest of the class. Make some notes below before presenting your findings.

1. How do you respond to the abrupt way in which Lady Capulet asks Juliet if she feels ready to accept a marriage proposal? What does she then reveal about her own experience? How close do you think she is to her daughter?
2. Look at Lady Capulet's description of Paris from 'Read o'er the volume ...'. Look at the words: *volume, writ, written, margent, unbound, cover, book of love, gold clasps*. What extended metaphor is being used here, and what aspects of Paris does Lady Capulet focus on?
3. What does Lady Capulet see the purpose of marriage as being for a young girl from a wealthy family? What does she want for her daughter's future?
4. What do you feel Juliet might be thinking or feeling at this point?

....

....

....

....

....

....

....

Extract 9.2.1 Act 1 Sc 5 — *'She doth teach the torches to burn bright!'*

The story continues ...

Capulet has sent his servant out with invitations to his feast. However, the servant cannot read. Out in the streets he sees Romeo and Benvolio and asks for their help. By way of thanks, he invites them to come to the feast, which is to be a masked event. That evening the young Montague men attend the lively Capulet feast and Romeo quickly forgets his past love when he catches sight of Juliet.

Romeo
O, she doth teach the torches to burn bright!
It seems she hangs upon the cheek of night
Like a rich jewel in an Ethiop's ear –
Beauty too rich for use, for earth too dear! 45
So shows a snowy dove trooping with crows
As yonder lady o'er her fellows shows.
The measure done, I'll watch her place of stand,
And, touching hers, make blessed my rude hand.
Did my heart love till now? Forswear it, sight; 50
For I ne'er saw true beauty till this night.

Tybalt
This, by his voice, should be a Montague.
Fetch me my rapier, boy. What, dares the slave
Come hither, cover'd with an **antic face**,
To fleer and scorn at our solemnity? 55
Now, by the stock and honour of my kin,
To strike him dead I hold it not a sin.

Capulet
Why, how now, kinsman! Wherefore storm you so?

Tybalt
Uncle, this is a Montague, our foe;
A villain, that is hither come in spite 60
To scorn at our solemnity this night.

Capulet
Young Romeo, is it?

Tybalt
'Tis he, that villain Romeo.

Capulet
Content thee, gentle coz, let him alone.
'A bears him like a **portly** gentleman;
And, to say truth, Verona brags of him 65
To be a virtuous and well-govern'd youth.
I would not for the wealth of all this town
Here in my house do him disparagement.
Therefore be patient, take no note of him;
It is my will; the which if thou respect, 70

Show a fair presence and put off these frowns,
And ill-beseeming semblance for a feast.

Tybalt

It fits, when such a villain is a guest.
I'll not endure him.

Capulet

He shall be endur'd:
What, goodman boy! I say, he shall. Go to; 75
Am I the master here or you? Go to.
You'll not endure him! God shall mend my soul!
You'll make a mutiny among my guests!
You will set cock-a-hoop! You'll be the man!

Tybalt

Why, uncle, 'tis a shame.

Capulet

Go to, go to; 80
You are **a saucy boy**. Is't so, indeed?
This trick may chance to scathe you. I know what:
You must contrary me. Marry, 'tis time. –
Well said, my hearts! – You are **a princox**; go.
Be quiet, or – More light, more light! – For shame! 85
I'll make you quiet. What! – Cheerly, my hearts!

Tybalt

Patience perforce with wilful **choler** meeting
Makes my flesh tremble in their different greeting.
I will withdraw; but this intrusion shall,
Now seeming sweet, convert to bitt'rest gall. 90

[Exit.]

Romeo

[To JULIET*]* If I profane with my unworthiest hand
This holy shrine, the gentle fine is this:
My lips, two blushing pilgrims, ready stand
To smooth that rough touch with a tender kiss.

Juliet

Good pilgrim, you do wrong your hand too much, 95
Which mannerly devotion shows in this;
For saints have hands that pilgrims' hands do touch,
And palm to palm is holy palmers' kiss.

Romeo

Have not saints lips, and holy palmers too?

Juliet

Ay, pilgrim, lips that they must use in pray'r. 100

Romeo

O, then, dear saint, let lips do what hands do!
They pray; grant thou, lest faith turn to despair.

Juliet

Saints do not move, though grant for prayers' sake.

Romeo	Then move not while my prayer's effect I take. Thus from my lips by thine my sin is purg'd.	105
	[Kissing her.]	
Juliet	Then have my lips the sin that they have took.	
Romeo	Sin from my lips? O trespass sweetly urg'd! Give me my sin again.	
	[Kissing her.]	
Juliet	You kiss by th' book.	
Nurse	Madam, your mother craves a word with you.	
Romeo	What is her mother?	
Nurse	Marry, bachelor, Her mother is the lady of the house, And a good lady, and a wise and virtuous. I nurs'd her daughter, that you talk'd withal. I tell you, he that can lay hold of her Shall have **the chinks**.	110
Romeo	Is she a Capulet? O dear account! my life is my foe's debt.	115

Glossary

the measure: the dance

antic face: a mask

portly: well mannered

a saucy boy: rude, insolent young man

princox: a rude person with too much to say

choler: anger

the chinks: a valuable treasure

Lesson 9.2.1 — *'She doth teach the torches to burn bright!'*

Learning objective(s):	Resources:
• To explore the initial meeting between Romeo and Juliet. • To consider the images of fate, religion and concealment used to present their initial meeting.	• PowerPoint 9.2.1 • Extract 9.2.1 • Worksheet 9.2.1

Getting started

- Distribute **Extract 9.2.1**. Use **The story continues …** to introduce the scene ahead. Share the lesson objectives on **PowerPoint slide 1** with the class and then display **PowerPoint slide 2**. Explain that this is Romeo's speech just ahead of his arrival at the Capulet feast. Working with the whole class, ask how they think Romeo is feeling about the night ahead. Ask what creates this impression. Draw attention to words connected with fate and explore the use of foreshadowing here. Draw attention to the noun phrases 'vile forfeit' and 'untimely death' as well as the adverb 'bitterly'. Ask students to think about how an actor might present this speech to communicate these feelings of foreboding and perhaps select one or two volunteers to read it out in role.

- Allocate parts and read aloud the extract from Act 1 Scene 5, presenting the Capulet feast and the initial meeting between Romeo and Juliet.

- To aid conceptualisation of the spectacle of this scene and the impact of the first meeting between the main protagonists, students could watch a version from a film or live production at this point.

Developing skills

- Display **PowerPoint slide 3** and ask students to work in pairs on the prompt questions, making notes in their notebooks or by annotating the extract. Allow time for the exploration and then take feedback from students, which should include: *1. Romeo's rapid change of heart showing his changeable and impetuous nature; 2. Tybalt's fiery temper and his focus on defending family honour, as well as his ability to respond to situations with violence; 3. Capulet keeps the peace and says Romeo should stay, noting that he has a reputation for being a well-behaved and honourable young man – explore the irony of how he could have made a perfect husband for Juliet and brought the families together; 4. Capulet, however, is focused on bringing about the match between Paris and Juliet and wants the feast to be a success.*

- Hand out **Worksheet 9.2.1** and ask students to work in small groups to complete **Activity 1**. Move among the groups, helping them to count out the rhyme scheme and recognise the use of the sonnet form here (3 × *abab* + the rhyming couplet) and the possible effect or impact of that choice by Shakespeare. In feedback, you could explore how this poetic form was conventionally used to present courtly love. Take suggestions from the groups about how they feel the characters are developing, particularly Juliet's reactions to Romeo when she is meant to be looking to Paris as a future husband.

Trying it yourself

- Appoint some readers to read the extract for **Activity 2** on the worksheet. Then ask students to work individually on the three questions, developing and consolidating ideas and making meaningful links and connections with prior learning. Encourage students, in question 1, to recognise how Juliet uses concealment when she tries to discover Romeo's identity. What does this tell us she is capable of? Make links between the earlier foreshadowing from Romeo and Juliet's foreshadowing now. Test recall by linking Juliet's words with Romeo's dialogue in Act 1 Scene 1: *'O brawling love! O loving hate!'*

Taking it further

- Use the prompt questions on **PowerPoint slide 4** with the class to explore the wider consequences of concealed identity. Discuss ideas around why Shakespeare chose to make the feast masked. How does this add to the tension and the mystery and make the meeting of the lovers more impactful?

- You may wish to ask students to prepare for the next lesson by bringing in a selection of their own art and craft materials, or prepare a selection of your own.

Worksheet 9.2.1 — 'She doth teach the torches to burn bright!'

Activity 1

Working in a small group, look closely at the exchange between Romeo and Juliet from when Romeo says: 'If I profane with my unworthiest hand/This holy shrine' to Juliet's line 'You kiss by th' book.'

1. How many words connected with religion can you find in this section? Make a list of them. In what way might this be seen as an extended metaphor and why might Romeo use this in relation to this meeting?
2. What do you notice about the pattern of rhyming words in this section and why might that be a deliberate choice by Shakespeare?
3. What do you notice about the first 14 lines of this exchange? What form is used here and why might that be a deliberate (and clever!) choice by Shakespeare?
4. What impression of Romeo is created from this exchange? How might this add to what we know already?
5. How does this exchange tell us more about Juliet? Who is she supposed to be 'looking to like' at the feast?
6. In what way is this fateful meeting connected to Romeo's feelings before the feast?

Activity 2

Read the extract below. This is from the end of the scene at the feast (Act 1 Scene 5) where the Nurse reveals their true identities to both Romeo and Juliet.

1. How does Juliet hide that she is interested in Romeo? What does this tell us about her character?
2. Write a paragraph in your notebook exploring what Juliet might be thinking and feeling when she says, 'My grave is like to be my wedding bed.' How does this connect with Romeo's feelings in the speech you explored before the party?
3. Can you recall and find a line spoken by Romeo earlier in Act 1 that has a direct connection with Juliet's line, 'My only love, sprung from my only hate!'?

Nurse
    Madam, your mother craves a word with you.

Romeo
    What is her mother?

Nurse
                                Marry, bachelor,   110
    Her mother is the lady of the house,
    And a good lady, and a wise and virtuous.
    I nurs'd her daughter, that you talk'd withal.
    I tell you, he that can lay hold of her
    Shall have the chinks.

Romeo

                                                                 Is she a Capulet?   115
O dear account! my life is my foe's debt.

Benvolio

Away, begone; the sport is at the best.

Romeo

Ay, so I fear; the more is my unrest.

Capulet

Nay, gentlemen, prepare not to be gone;
We have a trifling foolish banquet towards.   120
Is it e'en so? Why, then, I thank you all;
I thank you, honest gentlemen; good night.
More torches here! *[Exeunt* MASKERS*]* Come on then, let's to bed.
Ah, sirrah, by my fay, it waxes late;
I'll to my rest.   125

            [Exeunt all but JULIET *and* NURSE.*]*

Juliet

Come hither, nurse. What is yond gentleman?

Nurse

The son and heir of old Tiberio.

Juliet

What's he that now is going out of door?

Nurse

Marry, that I think be young Petruchio.

Juliet

What's he that follows there, that would not dance?   130

Nurse

I know not.

Juliet

Go ask his name. – If he be married,
My grave is like to be my wedding bed.

Nurse

His name is Romeo, and a Montague;
The only son of your great enemy.   135

Juliet

My only love sprung from my only hate!
Too early seen unknown, and known too late!
Prodigious birth of love it is to me,
That I must love a loathed enemy.

Lesson 9.2.2

'Too early seen unknown, and known too late!'

Learning objective(s):
- To create mask designs for Romeo and Juliet, symbolising their characters.

Resources:
- PowerPoint 9.2.2
- Extract 9.2.1
- Worksheet 9.2.2
- A selection of art and craft materials, sheets of cardboard to create masks
- Blank postcards or plain paper

It is useful to prepare art and craft materials for the worksheet before the lesson, or ask students in advance to bring materials to the lesson.

Recap and reflection

- Share the lesson objective on **PowerPoint slide 1** with the class. Then display **PowerPoint slide 2** and allow students some time to recap and reflect on what they have learned or understood so far about the characters of Romeo and Juliet, using the tasks on the slide to help them consolidate their knowledge. They could refer to **Extract 9.2.1** from the previous lesson. Take feedback and ideas from the class.

Developing skills

- Display **PowerPoint slide 3** and, working with the whole class, ask students to share ideas about the key images that might symbolise each character. Collate these ideas on the board. Suggestions might include symbols connected to love, the stars, the moon, fate, jewels, light, darkness, religion, prayer, marriage, death.

Trying it yourself

- Distribute **Worksheet 9.2.2** and allow time for students to use the template to create their mask designs for the two characters. Students could use the templates and cut out cardboard versions to be more substantial before adding their designs and decorations. Ensure that a range of art and craft materials are available.

Final task

- Display **PowerPoint slide 4**. Allow five to ten minutes at the end of the lesson for students to complete a commentary on their design choices using blank postcards or plain paper. You could use the masks and commentaries as part of a classroom display of work on the play.

Worksheet 9.2.2

'Too early seen unknown, and known too late!'

Activity

Create two designs for masks to be worn at the Capulet feast: one for Romeo and one for Juliet. Aim to incorporate symbols, details and decorations that would be appropriate for each character and reflect their language and use of imagery so far.

You could use the designs below as templates to cut out in card or use your own.

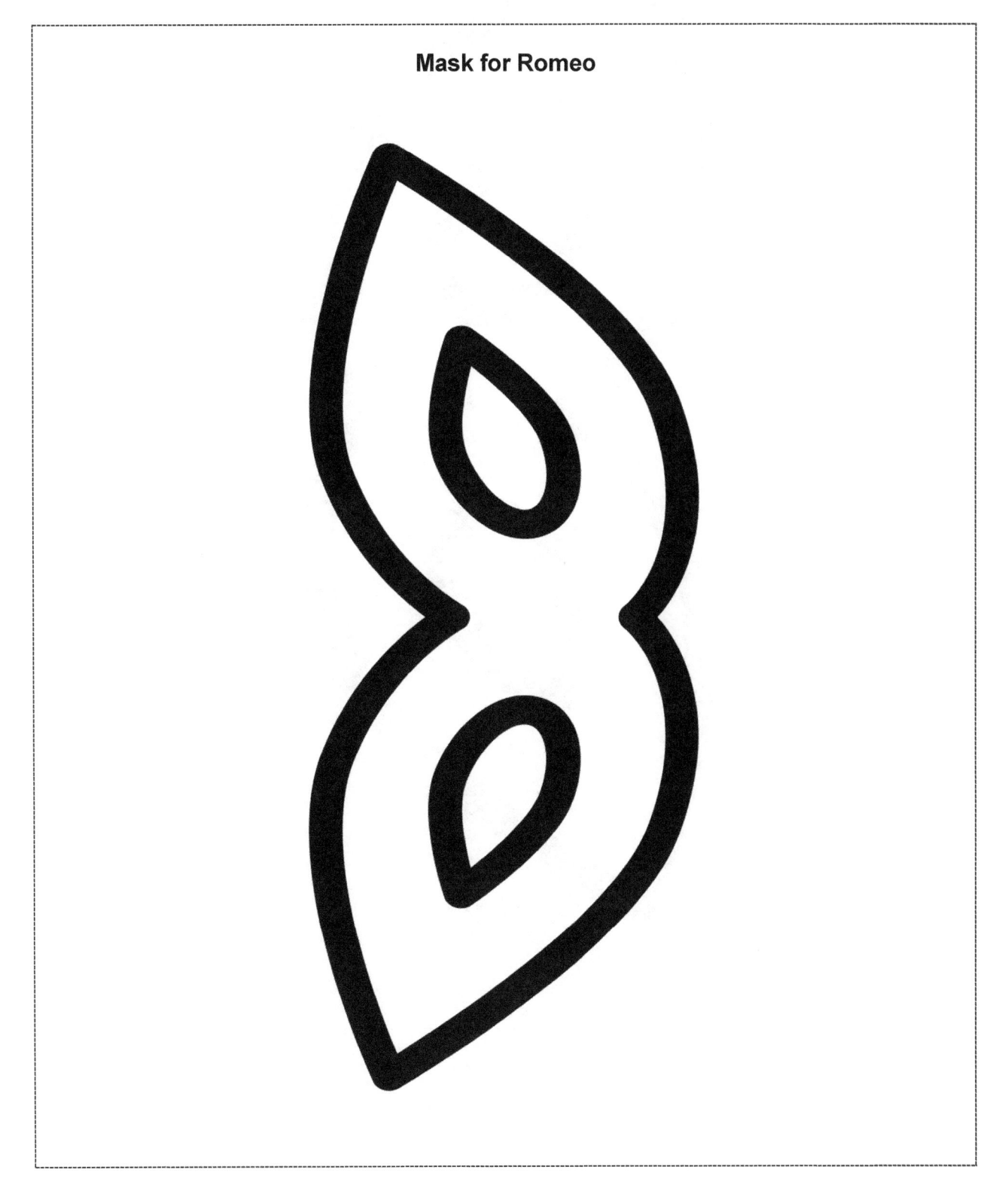

Mask for Romeo

Mask for Juliet

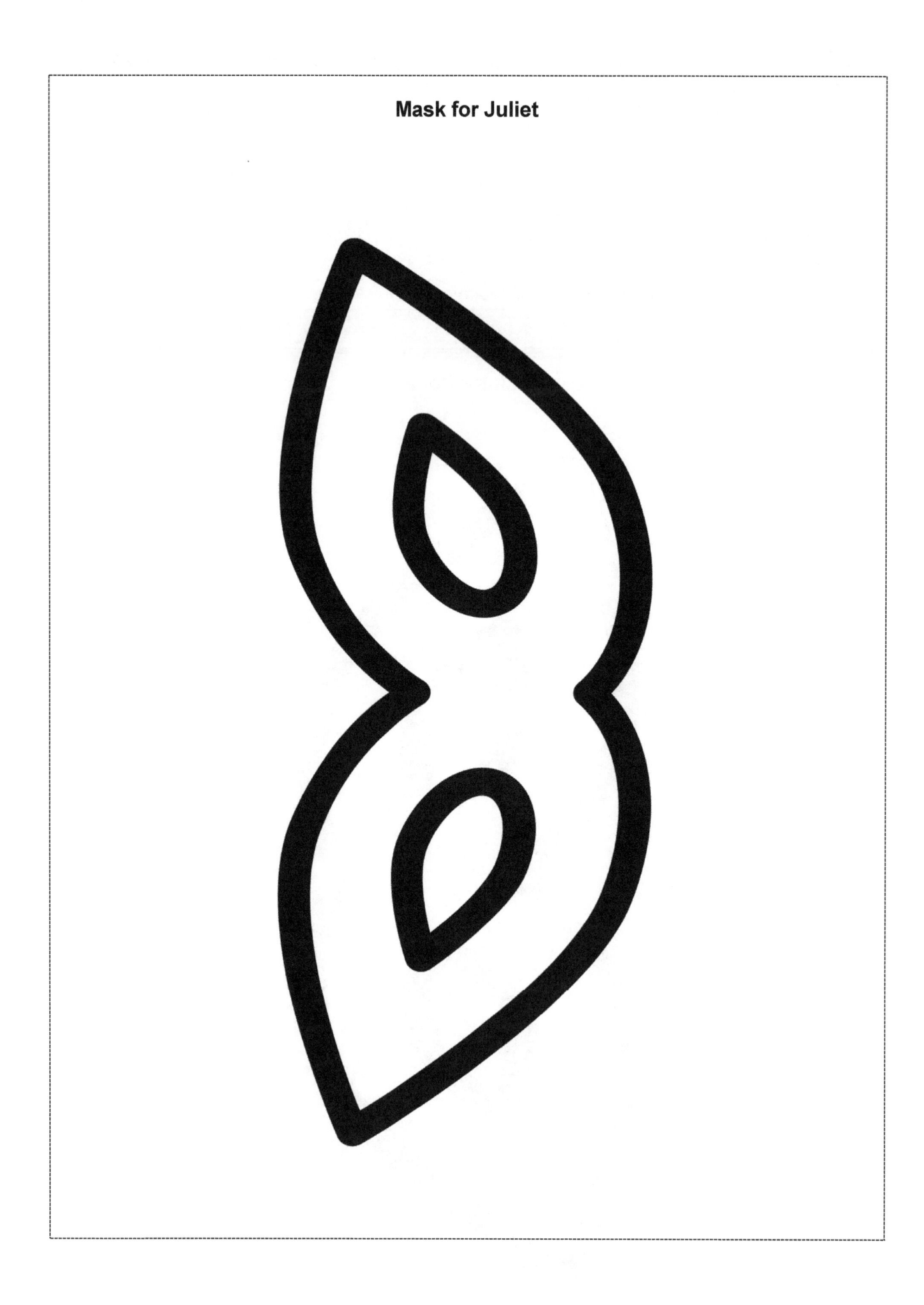

Extract 9.3.1
Act 2 Sc 2
'If thou dost love, pronounce it faithfully'

The story continues ...

As the Capulet feast ends and the guests depart, Romeo does not leave with his friends but climbs the walls of Capulet's orchard, desperate to see Juliet again. He sees her at her window.

Juliet

O Romeo, Romeo! **wherefore** art thou Romeo?
Deny thy father and refuse thy name;
Or, if thou wilt not, be but sworn my love, 35
And I'll no longer be a Capulet.

Romeo

[*Aside*] Shall I hear more, or shall I speak at this?

Juliet

'Tis but thy name that is my enemy;
Thou art thyself, though not a Montague.
What's Montague? It is nor hand, nor foot, 40
Nor arm, nor face, nor any other part
Belonging to a man. O, be some other name!
What's in a name? That which we call a rose
By any other name would smell as sweet;
So Romeo would, were he not Romeo call'd, 45
Retain that dear perfection which he owes
Without that title. Romeo, **doff** thy name;
And for thy name, which is no part of thee
Take all myself.

Romeo

I take thee at thy word:
Call me but love, and I'll be new baptiz'd; 50
Henceforth I never will be Romeo.

Juliet

What man art thou, that, thus **bescreen'd** in night,
So stumblest on my **counsel**?

Romeo

By a name
I know not how to tell thee who I am:
My name, dear saint, is hateful to myself, 55
Because it is an enemy to thee;
Had I it written, I would tear the word.

Juliet

My ears have not yet drunk a hundred words
Of that tongue's uttering, yet I know the sound:
Art thou not Romeo, and a Montague? 60

Romeo

    Neither, fair maid, if either thee dislike.

Juliet

    How cam'st thou hither, tell me, and wherefore?
    The orchard walls are high and hard to climb;
    And the place death, considering who thou art,
    If any of my kinsmen find thee here.   65

Romeo

    With love's light wings did I o'erperch these walls,
    For stony limits cannot hold love out;
    And what love can do, that dares love attempt.
    Therefore thy kinsmen are no stop to me.

Juliet

    If they do see thee, they will murder thee.   70

Romeo

    Alack, there lies more peril in thine eye
    Than twenty of their swords; look thou but sweet,
    And I am proof against their enmity.

Juliet

    I would not for the world they saw thee here.

Romeo

    I have night's cloak to hide me from their eyes;   75
    And but thou love me, let them find me here.
    My life were better ended by their hate
    Than death **prorogued** wanting of thy love.

Juliet

    By whose direction found'st thou out this place?

Romeo

    By love, who first did prompt me to enquire;   80
    He lent me counsel, and I lent him eyes.
    I am no pilot; yet, wert thou as far
    As that vast shore wash'd with the farthest sea,
    I should adventure for such merchandise.

Juliet

    Thou knowest the mask of night is on my face,   85
    Else would a maiden blush bepaint my cheek
    For that which thou hast heard me speak to-night.
    Fain would I dwell on form, fain, fain deny
    What I have spoke; but **farewell compliment**!
    Dost thou love me? I know thou wilt say ay,   90
    And I will take thy word; yet, if thou swear'st,
    Thou mayst prove false; at **lovers' perjuries**
    They say Jove laughs. O gentle Romeo,
    If thou dost love, pronounce it faithfully.
    Or, if thou think'st I am too quickly won,   95
    I'll frown, and be perverse, and say thee nay,
    So thou wilt woo; but else, not for the world.
    In truth, fair Montague, I am **too fond**;
    And therefore thou mayst **think my haviour light**;

But trust me, gentleman, I'll prove more true 100
Than those that have more cunning to be strange.
I should have been more strange, I must confess,
But that thou overheard'st, ere I was ware,
My true love's passion. Therefore pardon me,
And not impute this yielding to light love, 105
Which the dark night hath so discovered.

Romeo

Lady, by yonder blessed moon I vow,
That tips with silver all these fruit-tree tops –

Juliet

O, swear not by the moon, th' inconstant moon,
That monthly changes in her circled orb, 110
Lest that thy love prove likewise variable.

Romeo

What shall I swear by?

Juliet

Do not swear at all;
Or, if thou wilt, swear by thy gracious self,
Which is the god of my idolatry,
And I'll believe thee.

Romeo

If my heart's dear love – 115

Juliet

Well, do not swear. Although I joy in thee,
I have no joy of **this contract** to-night:
It is too rash, too unadvis'd, too sudden;
Too like the lightning, which doth cease to be
Ere one can say 'It lightens'. Sweet, good night! 120
This bud of love, by summer's ripening breath,
May prove a beauteous flow'r when next we meet.
Good night, good night! As sweet repose and rest
Come to thy heart as that within my breast!

Romeo

O, wilt thou leave me so unsatisfied? 125

Juliet

What satisfaction canst thou have to-night?

Romeo

Th' exchange of thy love's faithful vow for mine.

Juliet

I gave thee mine before thou didst request it;
And yet I would it were to give again.

Glossary

wherefore: why

doff: remove

bescreen'd: hidden

counsel: private thoughts

prorogued: delayed

farewell compliment: away with being formal

lovers' perjuries: lovers' lies

too fond: too foolish

think my haviour light: think I am being too forward (haviour = behaviour)

this contract: this vow

Lesson 9.3.1 — 'If thou dost love, pronounce it faithfully'

Learning objective(s):	Resources:
• To explore the development of Romeo and Juliet's relationship. • To consider the risks they are taking and the consequences of their decision to marry.	• PowerPoint 9.3.1 • Extract 9.3.1 • Worksheet 9.3.1

Getting started

- Begin this lesson by asking students to present some of their masks and commentaries from the previous lesson. Share the lesson objectives on **PowerPoint slide 1**, then display **PowerPoint slide 2** and use some of the students' thoughts on character to inform their thoughts on the question prompts on the slide.
- Distribute **Extract 9.3.1** and **Worksheet 9.3.1** and read aloud **The story continues …** for students.

Developing skills

- Organise students into small groups and direct them to **Activity 1** on the worksheet, which focuses on Romeo at the beginning of Act 2 Scene 2. Read aloud the extract for students or use an audio version online to aid comprehension of these longer speeches. Ask students to work in their groups to find and highlight the references to light and the rhetorical questions (remind them what these are) before annotating the extract with their collective ideas about what is implied about his feelings and how he sees Juliet. Ask students to draw some conclusions as to why they think he compares her to the sun, and take ideas and suggestions from each group as to their possible interpretations.
- Allocate two confident readers (or use an online audio version of this scene) to read **Extract 9.3.1** aloud.
- Organise students into pairs now to do a focused close reading of the extract using **Activity 2** on the worksheet, which moves students chronologically through the scene, exploring as they go. If time allows, you could take feedback from this exercise or take in student responses for formative assessment. They should have picked up on key points such as: *the fact that both lovers would reject their family name to be together; Romeo overhears Juliet talking of her feelings about him and suggesting she loves him despite his family being her family's enemies; Romeo is encouraged by this and feels he can speak out; Juliet is immediately worried for his safety and feels that he would be killed if her family found him there (contrast this with Capulet saying he should stay at the feast – which Juliet did not hear); Juliet is bold and direct about her feelings and does not reject Romeo like Rosaline; we see again how sensitive and respectful Romeo is when he makes a vow of love to her.*
- Display **PowerPoint slide 3** and tell students that this is the next part of the scene. Read the extract aloud and ask students what Juliet suggests to Romeo here. How do they respond to this? Consider how Juliet has just said that the situation was *'too rash, too unadvis'd, too sudden'*. What is also surprising about the fact that it is Juliet who asks Romeo here compared with what we saw earlier in the play when Paris visited Capulet? What is Juliet doing here? How unusual might it be that she takes control of her own future and happiness? What message might Shakespeare be giving us here?

Taking it further

- Display **PowerPoint slide 4** and ask students to consider the question prompts with a partner for a few minutes before taking ideas from the whole class. Take different opinions regarding how students respond to Romeo and Juliet's situation and its suddenness, and push for further consolidation of their thoughts. Do they believe the couple are genuinely in love? Do they believe in love at first sight? Is Juliet using this as a way of escaping her potential arranged marriage to Paris and controlling her own destiny? Ask students to reflect on the feud between the families. Should Romeo and Juliet be honest and open with their parents at this point? What might the advantages and disadvantages of this be? What might the consequences be of them keeping the relationship a secret, and what do we know about the repercussions of defending family honour in the play so far?

Worksheet 9.3.1 — 'If thou dost love, pronounce it faithfully'

Activity 1

Explore the extract below in a small group. It is from the opening of Act 2 Scene 2.

- How many different references to images of light can you find in Romeo's first two speeches below? What does this imply about how he sees Juliet?
- How many rhetorical questions does he ask? What does this tell us about how he is feeling?
- Why does he compare her to the sun and not the moon?

Romeo [...]
But, soft! What light through yonder window breaks
It is the east, and Juliet is the sun.
Arise, fair sun, and kill the envious moon,
Who is already sick and pale with grief   5
That thou her maid art far more fair than she.
Be not her maid, since she is envious;
Her vestal livery is but sick and green,
And none but fools do wear it; cast it off.
It is my lady; O, it is my love!   10
O that she knew she were!
She speaks, yet she says nothing. What of that?
Her eye discourses; I will answer it.
I am too bold, 'tis not to me she speaks;
Two of the fairest stars in all the heaven,   15
Having some business, do entreat her eyes
To twinkle in their spheres till they return.
What if her eyes were there, they in her head?
The brightness of her cheek would shame those stars,
As daylight doth a lamp; her eyes in heaven   20
Would through the airy region stream so bright
That birds would sing and think it were not night.
See how she leans her cheek upon her hand!
O that I were a glove upon that hand,
That I might touch that cheek!

Juliet
                          Ay me!

Romeo
                          She speaks.   25
O, speak again, bright angel, for thou art
As glorious to this night, being o'er my head,
As is a winged messenger of heaven
Unto the white-upturned wond'ring eyes
Of mortals that fall back to gaze on him,   30
When he bestrides the lazy-pacing clouds
And sails upon the bosom of the air.

Activity 2

Working with a partner, make detailed notes in your notebook or below for each of the following questions. Include a quotation from the extract to support each of your responses.

1. What does the early part of the scene tell us about how Romeo and Juliet feel about their family name? What does it seem they both want to do? Is it only their names that are the problem here? What other barriers stand in the way of them being together?
2. What is interesting about the fact that Romeo overhears what Juliet is saying as he hides in the orchard? What is he hearing and why does that give him the courage to speak out to her?
3. What risk has Romeo taken by climbing into the Capulet orchard? What warning does Juliet give him?
4. In what ways is Juliet different from what we have heard about Rosaline? Is she shy with Romeo? Does she hold back on expressing her feelings?
5. In what ways is Romeo different from the other young men of Verona who make rude and sexual jokes about women. How do we know that his intentions towards Juliet are honourable?

Extract 9.3.2a Act 2 Sc 3

'Wisely and slow; they stumble that run fast.'

The story continues ...

The next morning, Friar Lawrence is gathering herbs in his garden for remedies and potions. He reflects on how they are like people in that they can be used for good or evil purposes. Having said goodbye to Juliet, Romeo visits Friar Lawrence. The Friar notices that Romeo has been up all night.

Romeo
I'll tell thee ere thou ask it me again.
I have been feasting with mine enemy;
Where, on a sudden, one hath wounded me   50
That's by me wounded; both our remedies
Within thy help and holy physic lies.
I bear no hatred, blessed man, for, lo,
My **intercession** likewise steads my foe.

Friar Lawrence
Be plain, good son, and homely in thy drift;   55
Riddling confession finds but riddling shrift.

Romeo
Then plainly know my heart's dear love is set
On the fair daughter of rich Capulet.
As mine on hers, so hers is set on mine;
And all combin'd, save what thou must combine   60
By holy marriage. When, and where, and how,
We met, we woo'd, and made exchange of vow,
I'll tell thee as we pass; but this I pray,
That thou consent to marry us to-day.

Friar Lawrence
Holy Saint Francis. What a change is here!   65
Is Rosaline, that thou didst love so dear,
So soon forsaken? Young men's love, then, lies
Not truly in their hearts, but in their eyes.
Jesu Maria, what **a deal of brine**
Hath wash'd thy sallow cheeks for Rosaline!   70
How much salt water thrown away in waste,
To season love, that of it doth not taste!
The sun not yet thy sighs from heaven clears,
Thy old groans ring yet in my ancient ears;
Lo, here upon thy cheek the stain doth sit   75
Of an old tear that is not wash'd off yet.
If e'er thou wast thyself, and these woes thine,
Thou and these woes were all for Rosaline.
And art thou chang'd? Pronounce this sentence, then
Women may fall, when there's no strength in men.   80

Romeo
> Thou **chid'st** me oft for loving Rosaline.

Friar Lawrence
> For **doting**, not for loving, pupil mine.

Romeo
> And **bad'st me** bury love.

Friar Lawrence
> Not in a grave
> To lay one in, another out to have.

Romeo
> I pray thee chide me not; her I love now   85
> Doth grace for grace and love for love allow;
> The other did not so.

Friar Lawrence
> O, she knew well
> Thy love did read by rote that could not spell.
> But come, young waverer, come, go with me,
> In one respect I'll thy assistant be;   90
> For this alliance may so happy prove
> To turn your households' **rancour** to pure love.

Romeo
> O, let us hence; I stand on sudden haste.

Friar Lawrence
> Wisely and slow; they stumble that run fast.

Glossary

intercession: prayer

Riddling confession finds but riddling shrift: making a confusing confession will get you a confusing absolution

a deal of brine: a lot of tears

chid'st: told me off

doting: being infatuated

bad'st me: told me to

rancour: hatred

Extract 9.3.2b
Act 2 Sc 5

'Wisely and slow; they stumble that run fast.'

The story continues ...

Later the next morning, Juliet sends her Nurse to find Romeo as she promised she would do. The Nurse hears that Romeo has arranged for the Friar to perform the marriage ceremony that afternoon. Juliet waits impatiently for her return.

Nurse

    Jesu, what haste? Can you not stay awhile?
    Do you not see that I am out of breath? 30

Juliet

    How art thou out of breath, when thou hast breath
    To say to me that thou art out of breath?
    The excuse that thou dost make in this delay
    Is longer than the tale thou dost excuse.
    Is thy news good or bad? Answer to that; 35
    Say either, and I'll stay the circumstance.
    Let me be satisfied, is't good or bad?

Nurse

    Well, you have made a simple choice; you know not
    how to choose a man. Romeo! no, not he; though his
    face be better than any man's, yet his leg excels all 40
    men's; and for a hand, and a foot, and a body, though
    they be not to be talk'd on, yet they are past compare.
    He is not the flower of courtesy, but I'll warrant him
    as gentle as a lamb. Go thy ways, wench; serve God.
    What, have you din'd at home? 45

Juliet

    No, no. But all this did I know before.
    What says he of our marriage? What of that?

Nurse

    Lord, how my head aches! What a head have I!
    It beats as it would fall in twenty pieces.
    My back a t' other side – ah, my back, my back! 50
    Beshrew your heart for sending me about,
    To catch my death with jauncing up and down!

Juliet

    I' faith, I am sorry that thou art not well.
    Sweet, sweet, sweet nurse, tell me, what says my love?

Nurse

    Your love says, like an honest gentleman, and a courteous, 55
    and a kind, and a handsome, and, I warrant, a
    virtuous – Where is your mother?

Juliet

    Where is my mother! Why, she is within;
    Where should she be? How oddly thou repliest!

	'Your love says, like an honest gentleman,	60
	Where is your mother?'	
Nurse		
	O God's lady dear!	
	Are you so hot? Marry, come up, I **trow**;	
	Is this the **poultice** for my aching bones?	
	Henceforward, do your messages yourself.	
Juliet		
	Here's **such a coil**! Come, what says Romeo?	65
Nurse		
	Have you got leave to go to shrift to-day?	
Juliet		
	I have.	
Nurse		
	Then hie you hence to Friar Lawrence' cell;	
	There stays a husband to make you a wife.	
	Now comes the **wanton blood** up in your cheeks;	70
	They'll be in scarlet straight at any news.	
	Hie you to church; I must another way,	
	To fetch a ladder, by the which your love	
	Must climb **a bird's nest** soon when it is dark.	
	I am the drudge, and toil in your delight;	75
	But you shall **bear the burden** soon at night.	

Glossary

beshrew: curse

trow: believe, think or suppose

poultice: a comforting remedy

such a coil: a fuss

wanton blood: blush

a bird's nest: to Juliet's bedroom

bear the burden: a reference to sex

Lesson 9.3.2 — *'Wisely and slow; they stumble that run fast.'*

Learning objective(s):	Resources:
• To understand the thoughts and actions of the Friar and the Nurse. • To explore how Shakespeare uses imagery to create the rising action.	• PowerPoint 9.3.2 • Extracts 9.3.2a; 9.3.2b

Recap and reflection

- Share the lesson objectives on **PowerPoint slide 1** with the class. Ask students to think back over their viewpoints from the final task in the last lesson and consider these in relation to the title of this lesson. What might this key quotation, which has the qualities of a proverb, imply? What swift change of heart did we see from Juliet in the previous lesson and what were the possible reasons for it? Distribute **Extract 9.3.2a**.

Developing skills

- Read aloud **The story continues …** and appoint two students to read aloud the roles of the Friar and Romeo. After the reading, display **PowerPoint slide 2** and ask students to work in pairs on the task on the slide. Suggest that students use the white space on the extract to draw large thought bubbles and then discuss the Friar's possible thoughts, feelings and changing reactions at each point. You could use a film or live production version of this scene in feedback to monitor the actor's reactions and check that students have picked up on the key ideas. Students should grasp that: *the Friar is initially confused; he is shocked and astounded that Romeo has forgotten all about Rosaline after his previous lovesick behaviour; he wasn't expecting him to find someone else so swiftly; he can see this might be a positive thing to bring the two feuding families together; Romeo should not act hastily nonetheless.*

- Display **PowerPoint slide 3** and, working with the whole class, pose the 'On the surface …' statements against the 'However …' questions. Take ideas and responses in a whole-class question and answer session to check students' knowledge recall and deeper thinking across the play so far. Prompt students to think about Romeo's friends and parents; that Friar Lawrence does not know about the suit from Paris to Juliet's father.

- Distribute **Extract 9.3.2b** and ask two students to read aloud the roles of Juliet and the Nurse.

Trying it yourself

- Display **PowerPoint slide 4** and ask students to work independently on these tasks, recording their answers in their notebooks. Question 1 sets up a retrieval task and asks for students' inferences. Question 2 invites students to recall prior learning and reflect on Juliet's situation and the risks she highlighted to Romeo of him being found in the orchard. Question 3 invites students to think more critically and explain their own opinions.

Final task

- Display **PowerPoint slide 5** and explain that these are the Friar's words just before he leads Romeo and Juliet into church to marry them (Act 2 Scene 6). Ask students what key images are used in the speech. What figurative language techniques can they identify to create each image? What do students think of or feel or imagine as they visualise the imagery? What seems to be the tone here? Ensure that students pick up on the ideas of risk, danger and explosive outcomes that are foreshadowed here, as well as the warnings about haste – though this is steeped in irony given that the Friar has agreed to the hasty marriage.

Taking it further

- It may be useful for students to see Act 2 in its entirety from a film or live performance to conceptualise the ideas raised in the last two lessons, before moving on. Additionally, a reciprocal read of Act 2 Scene 6 from pages 117 to 119 in the *Collins Classroom Classics* edition would consolidate the plot at this point.

Extract 9.4.1a Act 3 Sc 1 — 'And fire-ey'd fury be my conduct now!'

The story continues ...
Tybalt wants to fight Romeo for being at Lord Capulet's party.

A public place

[Enter MERCUTIO, BENVOLIO, PAGE, and SERVANTS.]

[...]

[Enter TYBALT and OTHERS.]

Benvolio
By my head, here comes the Capulets.

Mercutio
By my heel, I care not. 35

Tybalt
Follow me close, for I will speak to them.
Gentlemen, good den; a word with one of you.

Mercutio
And but one word with one of us? Couple it with
something; make it a word and a blow.

Tybalt
You shall find me apt enough to that, sir, an you will 40
give me occasion.

Mercutio
Could you not take some occasion without giving?

Tybalt
Mercutio, thou **consortest** with Romeo.

Mercutio
Consort! What, dost thou make us **minstrels**? An thou
make minstrels of us, look to hear nothing but 45
discords. Here's my **fiddlestick**; here's that shall make
you dance. **Zounds**, consort!

Benvolio
We talk here in the public haunt of men;
Either withdraw unto some private place,
Or reason coldly of your grievances, 50
Or else depart; here all eyes gaze on us.

Mercutio
Men's eyes were made to look, and let them gaze;
I will not budge for no man's pleasure, I.

Glossary

consortest: spending a lot of time with; Mercutio takes it as an insult that he is accused of spending a lot of time with minstrels

minstrels: travelling musicians

fiddlestick: sword

Zounds: 'God's wounds' – a violent oath

Extract 9.4.1b Act 3 Sc 1 — 'And fire-ey'd fury be my conduct now!'

The story continues ...
Romeo, having just wed Juliet, refuses to fight Tybalt. Mercutio steps in.

[Enter ROMEO.]

Tybalt
Well, peace be with you, sir. Here comes my man.

[...]

Romeo, the love I bear thee can afford
No better term than this: thou art a villain.

Romeo
Tybalt, the reason that I have to love thee   60
Doth much excuse the **appertaining rage**
To such a greeting. Villain am I none;
Therefore, farewell; I see thou know'st me not.

Tybalt
Boy, this shall not excuse the injuries
That thou hast done me; therefore turn and draw.   65

Romeo
I do protest I never injur'd thee,
But love thee better than thou canst **devise**
Till thou shalt know the reason of my love;
And so, good Capulet – which name I tender
As dearly as mine own – be satisfied.   70

Mercutio
O calm, dishonourable, vile submission!
[...] [Draws]
Tybalt, you rat-catcher, will you walk?

[...]

Tybalt
I am for you. *[Draws]*

Romeo
Gentle Mercutio, put thy **rapier** up.

Mercutio
Come, sir, your **passado**. *[They fight]*

[...]

[TYBALT under ROMEO'S arm thrusts MERCUTIO in, and flies with his friends.]

Mercutio

I am hurt.
A plague a both your houses!

[...]

They have made worms' meat of me. 105
I have it, and soundly too – Your houses!

[Exeunt MERCUTIO and BENVOLIO.]

Glossary

appertaining rage: natural anger

devise: realise

rapier: a type of sword

passado: thrust with a sword, as in fencing

Extract 9.4.1c Act 3 Sc 1 — 'And fire-ey'd fury be my conduct now!'

The story continues ...
The news of Mercutio's death makes Romeo seek revenge.

Romeo
> This gentleman, the Prince's near ally,
> My very friend, hath got this mortal hurt
> In my behalf; ... O sweet Juliet,
> Thy beauty hath made me **effeminate**,
> And in my temper soften'd valour's steel!

[Re-enter BENVOLIO.]

Benvolio
> O Romeo, Romeo, brave Mercutio is dead!

[...]

Romeo
> This day's black fate on moe days doth depend;
> This but begins the woe others must end.

[Re-enter TYBALT.]

Benvolio
> Here comes the furious Tybalt back again.

Romeo
> Alive in triumph and Mercutio slain!   120
> Away to heaven **respective lenity**,
> And fire-ey'd fury be my conduct now!
> Now, Tybalt, take the 'villain' back again
> That late thou gav'st me; for Mercutio's soul
> Is but a little way above our heads,   125
> Staying for thine to keep him company.
> Either thou or I, or both, must go with him.

Tybalt
> Thou, wretched boy, that didst consort him here,
> Shall with him hence.

Romeo
> This shall determine that.

[They fight: TYBALT falls.]

Benvolio
> Romeo, away, be gone.   130
> The citizens are up, and Tybalt slain.
> Stand not amaz'd. The Prince will doom thee death
> If thou art taken. Hence, be gone, away!

Romeo
> O, I am fortune's fool!

[…]
[Exit ROMEO.]

Glossary
effeminate: like a woman (without aggression)
respective lenity: respect and gentleness

Extract 9.4.1d Act 3 Sc 1: 'And fire-ey'd fury be my conduct now!'

The story continues ...
Romeo has fled and Tybalt lies dead.

[Enter PRINCE, attended: MONTAGUE. CAPULET, their WIVES, and all.]

Prince
Where are the vile beginners of this fray?

Benvolio
O noble Prince, **I can discover all** 140
The unlucky manage of this fatal brawl:
There lies the man, slain by young Romeo,
That slew thy kinsman, brave Mercutio.

Lady Capulet
Tybalt, my cousin! O my brother's child!
O Prince! O husband! O, the blood is spill'd 145
Of my dear kinsman! Prince, as thou art true,
For blood of ours shed blood of Montague.
O cousin, cousin!

Prince
Benvolio, who began this bloody fray?

Benvolio
Tybalt, here slain, whom Romeo's hand did slay; 150

[...]

Lady Capulet
He is a kinsman to the Montague,
Affection makes him false, he speaks not true; 175
Some twenty of them fought in this black strife,
And all those twenty could but kill one life.
I beg for justice, which thou. Prince, must give:
Romeo slew Tybalt, Romeo must not live.

Prince
Romeo slew him; he slew Mercutio. 180
Who now the price of his dear blood doth owe?

Montague
Not Romeo, Prince; he was Mercutio's friend;
His fault concludes but what the law should end,
The life of Tybalt.

Prince
And for that offence,
Immediately we do exile him hence. 185

Glossary
I can discover all: I can tell you all about it

Lesson 9.4.1 — *'And fire-ey'd fury be my conduct now!'*

Learning objective(s):	Resources:
• To understand how a scene is structured. • To explore key moments through freeze frames.	• PowerPoint 9.4.1 • Extracts 9.4.1a–d • Worksheet 9.4.1

Getting started

- Share the lesson objectives on **PowerPoint slide 1** with the class. Then organise students into four groups and hand out **Extracts 9.4.1a–d**, with all the students in each group having the same extract. Allocate the parts for students to read out or watch a video of Act 3 Scene 1. Use **The story so far …** and the glossaries to consolidate knowledge.

- Display **PowerPoint slide 2** and use the prompt questions to encourage students to think about the scene. Take responses from the class to develop understanding. Some ideas to consider: *the action is fast-paced and exciting, contrasting with the mood and pace at the end of Act 2; the action creates a turning point in the play – Romeo's reaction turns the hope and optimism of the marriage to despair; Romeo changes his behaviour from trying to keep the peace to becoming impulsive and hot-headed – his closest friend has been killed – if only he had fought Tybalt in the first place.*

Developing skills

- Display **PowerPoint slide 3**. Hand out **Worksheet 9.4.1** and get students back into their groups from the beginning of the lesson, each with their allocated extract. In large classes, two groups could work on the same scene. Ask students to complete **Activity 1** and **Activity 2** on the worksheet, creating a series of freeze frames that focus on their assigned extracts from Act 3 Scene 1.

- Allow time for students to plan and prepare, then ask groups to enact the extract through their series of freeze frames. Remind students to think carefully about how to move from one moment to another, without using dialogue. They should focus on gesture and facial expression to communicate the action and the feelings of the characters. Make sure each group starts and ends with a freeze frame.

Trying it yourself

- Display **PowerPoint slide 4**. In your performance space, get ready to watch each group's work. Choose whether to see every group or just a few. Remind students that when we watch others perform, we watch and listen carefully, without interrupting the performance. When each group performs, ensure that the audience can see each series of freeze frames clearly.

- After each performance, consider: Which key moments did the group capture? Which gestures and facial expressions did they use? How did these help us to understand the action? How do these key moments help us to understand the play as a whole?

- Ask students to complete **Activity 3** on **Worksheet 9.4.1**, reflecting on their own participation and performance choices.

Taking it further

- Follow up with a reciprocal reading lesson from pages 137 to 169 in the *Collins Classroom Classics* edition to consolidate the situation that Romeo and Juliet find themselves in and/or watch a version of these scenes to establish the key emotions at play.

Worksheet 9.4.1: 'And fire-ey'd fury be my conduct now!'

Activity 1

Read through your assigned extract from Act 3 Scene 1. Notice how the action develops in the scene.

Activity 2

In your group, create a series of freeze frames that focus on your extract.

Remember:

- You will need to think carefully about how to move from one freeze frame to another without using dialogue.
- You will need to focus on gesture and facial expression to communicate the action and feelings of the characters.

Activity 3

Evaluate the success of your group task by answering the questions below.

What did you think Shakespeare wanted the audience to focus on in this extract?

....

....

....

....

How did you decide which key moments to include?

....

....

....

....

Which expressions and gestures were the most successful? Why?

....

....

....

....

Extract 9.4.2
Act 3 Sc 5
'I would the fool were married to her grave!'

The story continues ...

Juliet receives the news of her cousin's death at the hand of Romeo. Although distraught, her love for Romeo means she wants to say goodbye before he is banished. Meanwhile, Capulet makes final arrangements for Juliet's marriage to Paris and Romeo spends his final night with his new wife. In this scene, Capulet and Lady Capulet bring the news of the wedding to their daughter.

[Enter LADY CAPULET.]

Lady Capulet
Why, how now, Juliet!

Juliet
Madam, I am not well.

Lady Capulet
Evermore weeping for your cousin's death?

[...]

Juliet
Feeling so the loss,
I cannot choose but ever weep the friend.

Lady Capulet
Well, girl, thou weep'st not so much for his death
As that the villain lives which slaughtered him.

Juliet
What villain, madam?

Lady Capulet
That same villain, Romeo.   80

[...]

But now I'll tell thee joyful tidings, girl.

[...]

Marry, my child, early next Thursday morn
The gallant, young, and noble gentleman,
The County Paris, at Saint Peter's Church,
Shall happily make thee there a joyful bride.   115

[...]

Juliet
[...] I pray you tell my lord and father, madam,
I will not marry yet; and when I do, I swear
It shall be Romeo, whom you know I hate,
Rather than Paris. These are news indeed!

[...]

[Enter CAPULET and Nurse.]

Capulet
>*[...]* How now! a **conduit**, girl? What, still in tears?
>*[...]* How now, wife!
>Have you delivered to her our **decree**?

Lady Capulet
>Ay, sir; but she will none, she gives you thanks.
>I would the fool were married to her grave!   140

Capulet
>*[...]* How will she none? Doth she not give us thanks?
>*[...]* Unworthy as she is, that we have wrought
>So worthy a gentleman to be her bridegroom?   145

[...]

>*[...]* **fettle your fine joints** 'gainst Thursday next,
>To go with Paris to Saint Peter's Church,
>Or I will drag thee on a **hurdle** thither.
>Out, you green-sickness **carrion**! Out, you baggage!
>You **tallow-face**!

[...]

Juliet
>Good father, I beseech you on my knees,
>Hear me with patience but to speak a word.

Capulet
>Hang thee, young baggage! disobedient wretch!   160
>I tell thee what – get thee to church a Thursday,
>Or never after look me in the face.
>Speak not, reply not, do not answer me;
>**My fingers itch**. Wife, we scarce thought us blest
>That God had lent us but this only child;   165
>But now I see this one is one too much,
>And that we have a curse in having her.
>Out on her, **hilding**!

[...]

Lady Capulet
>   You are too hot.   175

Capulet
>God's bread! it makes me mad:
>*[...]* Thursday is near; lay hand on heart, advise:
>An you be mine, I'll give you to my friend;
>An you be not, hang, beg, starve, die in the streets,
>For, by my soul, I'll ne'er acknowledge thee,
>Nor what is mine shall never do thee good.   195
>Trust to't, bethink you, I'll not be forsworn.

[Exit.]

Juliet

[...] O, sweet my mother, cast me not away!
Delay this marriage for a month, a week; 200
Or, if you do not, make the bridal bed
In that dim monument where Tybalt lies.

Lady Capulet

Talk not to me, for I'll not speak a word;
Do as thou wilt, for I have done with thee.

[Exit.]

Glossary

conduit: water pipe

decree: decision, order

fettle your fine joints: get yourself ready

hurdle: a wooden frame used to pull traitors through the streets

carrion: dead meat

tallow-face: pale-faced

my fingers itch: suggests Capulet is about to hit Juliet

hilding: a useless, broken-down horse; worthless

Lesson 9.4.2 — *'I would the fool were married to her grave!'*

Learning objective(s):	Resources:
• To explore the wider themes and issues of the play.	• PowerPoint 9.4.2
• To debate ideas using Forum Theatre.	• Extract 9.4.2
	• Worksheet 9.4.2

Recap and reflection

- Share the lesson objectives on **PowerPoint slide 1** with the class, then display **PowerPoint slide 2**. Revisit what students remember about the themes in the play. Ask them to do this individually. Set a timer for two minutes. Students could use whiteboards to record their responses. Then take feedback in a class discussion and get students to mark their own work. Some of the themes are: *love and hate; religion; family honour; fate.* Accept any sensible answer within these broader themes.

Developing skills

- Hand out **Extract 9.4.2** and read through it as a class, using the scene and the glossary to consolidate knowledge.

- Explain that students are going to develop their ideas from the **Recap and reflection** activity to explore different characters' points of view in **Extract 9.4.2** through Forum Theatre, a type of interactive drama that explores real-life issues. As students are exploring/enacting the scene, other group members should be able to stop the action at any point and step into the scene to play out different outcomes. Forum Theatre enables groups to investigate different arguments and points of view. For example, the first time they play out a debate, it may be from Juliet's point of view; the second time from Capulet's perspective. For further information, look up 'Augusto Boal' and the 'Theatre of the Oppressed'.

- Organise students into groups of three or four. Explain that each student in the group should take on one of these roles: Juliet; Lady Capulet; Capulet. If there is an even number of students in the group, the final role might be debate host/interviewer. Hand out **Worksheet 9.4.2** and instruct students to assign roles according to the guidance in **Activity 1**.

- Ask students to prepare to use Forum Theatre to debate one of the following: 1. Children should always obey their parents. 2. People should be free to choose who they want to marry. 3. Money and status are more important than love. Encourage students to be inventive and prepare their debate in the form of a family discussion, TV show or a more formal situation, such as in court. Tell students they are free to be creative. Work with groups to give shape and focus to the drama.

- Display **PowerPoint Slide 3**. Make sure students use persuasive techniques to formulate arguments and that they are familiar with the terminology. These might include emotive language; use of eye contact; rhetorical questions; direct address; anecdotes. No individual should speak for more than a minute.

Taking it further

- Display **PowerPoint slide 4**. In your performance space, get ready to watch each debate. Remind students that when we watch other people, we watch and listen carefully without interrupting. When each group speaks, ensure that the audience can hear the arguments clearly.

- After each performance, ask the rest of the class to give feedback on which character gave the strongest argument. They should also be prepared to justify their opinion and say how the situation might be resolved.

Final task

- Ask students to complete **Activity 2** on **Worksheet 9.4.2**, reflecting on their own participation and techniques used.

Taking it further

- Read to the end of Act 3 scene 5. Focus on Juliet's reactions and consider what the outcome of this scene now means for the plan Friar Lawrence has put in place. It may be worth watching a version of this scene in its entirety.

Worksheet 9.4.2 — 'I would the fool were married to her grave!'

Activity 1

- Prepare to debate one of the following, in role as one of these characters: Juliet, Lady Capulet, Capulet.
- Use one of these arguments to start your debate:
  1. Children should always obey their parents.
  2. People should be free to choose who they want to marry.
  3. Money and status are more important than love.
- Your character has one minute to put their point of view across. Make sure your character uses persuasive devices, such as: emotive language; eye contact; rhetorical questions; direct address; anecdote.
- You could get creative with your debate, giving it the form of a family discussion, or as a more formal situation, such as in court.

Activity 2

Evaluate the success of your argument, using the prompt questions below.

Which role did you take? ....

What persuasive techniques did you use to argue your point of view?

....
....
....
....
....
....

What advice would you give the characters to resolve the issues raised in the debate?

....
....
....
....
....

Extract 9.5.1
Act 4 Sc 1
'past hope, past cure, past help'

The story continues ...

Juliet, desperate following the news that she is to be married to Paris, hurries to Friar Lawrence for help. There she meets Paris who asks her to confirm that she loves him. She avoids answering him and he leaves, believing she wants to pray with the Friar.

Juliet
    O, shut the door, and when thou hast done so,
    Come weep with me – past hope, past cure, past help.   45

Friar Lawrence
    O, Juliet, I already know thy grief;
    It strains me past the compass of my wits.
    I hear thou must, and nothing may **prorogue** it,
    On Thursday next be married to this County.

Juliet
    Tell me not, friar, that thou hear'st of this,   50
    Unless thou tell me how I may prevent it;
    If, in thy wisdom, thou canst give no help,
    Do thou but call my resolution wise,
    And with this knife I'll help it presently.
    God join'd my heart and Romeo's, thou our hands;   55
    And ere this hand, by thee to Romeo seal'd,
    Shall be the label to another deed,
    Or my true heart with treacherous revolt
    Turn to another, this shall slay them both.
    Therefore, out of thy long-experienc'd time,   60
    Give me some present counsel; or, behold,
    'Twixt my extremes and me this bloody knife
    Shall play the umpire, arbitrating that
    Which **the commission of thy years** and art
    Could to no issue of true honour bring.   65
    Be not so long to speak; I long to die,
    If what thou speak'st speak not of remedy.

Friar Lawrence
    Hold, daughter; I do spy a kind of hope,
    Which craves as desperate an execution
    As that is desperate which we would prevent.   70
    If, rather than to marry County Paris,
    Thou hast the strength of will to slay thyself,
    Then is it likely thou wilt undertake
    A thing like death to chide away this shame,
    That cop'st with death himself to scape from it;   75
    And, if thou dar'st, I'll give thee remedy.

Juliet
    O, bid me leap, rather than marry Paris,
    From off the battlements of any tower,
    Or walk in thievish ways, or bid me lurk
    Where serpents are; chain me with roaring bears,   80

          Or hide me nightly in a **charnel house**,
          O'er-cover'd quite with dead men's rattling bones,
          With **reeky shanks** and yellow chapless skulls;
          Or bid me go into a new-made grave,
          And hide me with a dead man in his shroud –   85
          Things that, to hear them told, have made me tremble
          And I will do it without fear or doubt,
          To live an unstain'd wife to my sweet love.

Friar Lawrence
          Hold, then; go home, be merry, give consent
          To marry Paris. Wednesday is to-morrow;   90
          To-morrow night look that thou lie alone,
          Let not thy nurse lie with thee in thy chamber.
          Take thou this **vial**, being then in bed,
          And this distilled liquor drink thou off;
          When presently through all thy veins shall run   95
          A cold and drowsy humour; for no pulse
          Shall keep his native progress, but **surcease**;
          No warmth, no breath, shall testify thou livest;
          The roses in thy lips and cheeks shall fade
          To paly ashes, thy eyes' windows fall,   100
          Like death when he shuts up the day of life;
          Each part, depriv'd of **supple government**,
          Shall, stiff and stark and cold, appear like death;
          And in this borrow'd likeness of shrunk death
          Thou shalt continue two and forty hours,   105
          And then awake as from a pleasant sleep.
          Now, when the bridegroom in the morning comes
          To rouse thee from thy bed, there art thou dead.
          Then, as the manner of our country is,
          In thy best robes, uncovered on the bier,   110
          Thou shalt be borne to that same ancient vault
          Where all the kindred of the Capulets lie.
          In the meantime, against thou shalt awake,
          Shall Romeo by my letters know our drift,
          And hither shall he come; and he and I   115
          Will watch thy waking, and that very night
          Shall Romeo bear thee hence to Mantua.
          And this shall free thee from this present shame,
          If no inconstant toy nor womanish fear
          Abate thy valour in the acting it.   120

Glossary

prorogue: delay

the commission of thy years: your wisdom

charnel house: a store of human bones

reeky shanks: rotting legbones

vial: small bottle

surcease: stop

supple government: movement

Lesson 9.5.1 — *'past hope, past cure, past help'*

Learning objective(s):	**Resources:**
• To explore the language and imagery as Juliet faces a desperate situation. • To understand the Friar's plan.	• PowerPoint 9.5.1 • Extract 9.5.1 • Worksheet 9.5.1

Getting started

- Share the lesson objectives on **PowerPoint slide 1** with the class. Give out **Extract 9.5.1** and read aloud **The story so far …**. Display **PowerPoint slide 2** and discuss the opening of Act 4 where Paris shares the news with the Friar of his impending marriage to Juliet. Use the prompt questions on the slide with the whole class to explore possibilities. What has changed Capulet's mind about waiting two more summers for Juliet to be a bride? Explore the impact of the most recent street fight and the deaths of Tybalt and Mercutio. Is Capulet worried he will lose Paris as a suitor for Juliet? What is the irony of this? Explore with students the dramatic irony here of the Friar's position in knowing that Juliet is already married. What situation does this place him in?

Developing skills

- Display **PowerPoint slide 3** and appoint two readers to present the exchange between Paris and Juliet (Act 4 Scene 1). Ask students to comment on how this exchange is different from when we saw Romeo and Juliet together. What were their exchanges like compared with these? Encourage students to note the clipped responses. How do students respond to Paris's assertion that 'Thy face is mine.' How does this link to how Capulet referred to Juliet in the previous act?

- Appoint two readers to read **Extract 9.5.1** up to Juliet's line 'To live an unstain'd wife to my sweet love.'

- Hand out **Worksheet 9.5.1**. Ask students to work in pairs to complete **Activity 1** by exploring Juliet's speech. Suggest that they annotate their extract for questions 1 and 2 to show their findings and then 'think, pair, share' their inferential responses for question 3.

- Take some feedback to consolidate understanding, aiming for students to have understood the level of panic Juliet is feeling at this point and her sense of desperation; point out the number of references which help us to see that she views marriage to Paris as horrifying. Challenge students to think about the religious aspect of her marriage to Romeo – that Juliet's faith would have been Roman Catholic and to marry again when she has been married in the sight of God would be a sin. The Friar would also, clearly, have been aware of this.

Trying it yourself

- Read aloud Friar Lawrence's long speech for students beginning 'Hold, then; go home …', or you could make use of an online audio recording. Ask students to work individually on **Activity 2**, which takes them chronologically through the Friar's plan in an accessible way. Tell students that their answers will be used in the next lesson.

Taking it further

- Display **PowerPoint slide 4** and use the prompt questions to take different critical viewpoints from around the class regarding students' feelings about Juliet. Has she made wise choices? Was she right to follow her heart and make her own decisions? Should she have listened to her father or even approached him first? How do students respond to her moral dilemma with Paris? Does anyone have any sympathy for Paris at this point who, after all, has followed convention? Ask students to think now about the serious consequences of the help the Friar and the Nurse have given these young people. What are students' reactions to the dangerous and risky plan the Friar has now come up with – is he doing this purely for Juliet?

Worksheet 9.5.1 — 'past hope, past cure, past help'

Activity 1

With a partner, look closely at Juliet's speech beginning 'O, *bid me leap, ...*'.

1. How many different words or phrases can you find, which create an image of a horror story or nightmare? Circle them.
2. Look at the construction of Juliet's sentence. How many different ideas and alternatives does it contain? What does this seem to tell you about the pace at which she is speaking? What does this tell you about her state of mind?
3. What are Juliet's feelings about a marriage to Paris?

Challenge:

Juliet refers to God in her earlier speech. Why is this second marriage problematic from a religious point of view?

Activity 2

Answer the questions below to help you understand the Friar's plan to help Juliet.

1. List three things the Friar asks Juliet to do straight away.

    1. .... 2. .... 3. ....

2. What are Juliet's instructions for Wednesday night? Explain in clear statement sentences.

   ....

   ....

3. What are the different effects the potion will have on Juliet? ....

   ....

   ....

4. How long will the potion last? ....

5. What does the Friar anticipate will happen when her family find her 'dead' body? ....

   ....

   ....

6. What will the Friar be doing in the meantime? ....

   ....

   ....

Lesson 9.5.2

'Shall I be married, then, to-morrow morning?'

Learning objective(s):
- To reflect on the key ingredients of Shakespeare's plot.
- To recast the ingredients in a short story.

Resources:
- PowerPoint 9.5.2
- Worksheets 9.5.1 and 9.5.2

Recap and reflection

- Ask students to look at their responses to **Activity 2** on **Worksheet 9.5.1** from the last lesson and check the key aspects of Friar Lawrence's plan. Reflect on the effects of the potion he has created and how this will affect Juliet and create the semblance that she is dead. Share ideas as to how she might be feeling about this plan and how desperate she must be to go through with it.

- Display **PowerPoint slide 2** and read aloud Juliet's speech when Lady Capulet leaves her room and Juliet is alone the night before her second wedding. Explore the moment with the whole class. Ask students to think about the questions Juliet asks. What do they reveal of her anxieties at this point? What does the dagger imply? Aim to conclude whether students feel Juliet is being courageous or foolish to go through with the plan.

- Share the lesson objectives on **PowerPoint slide 1** with the class.

Developing skills

- Display **PowerPoint slide 3** and read Shakespeare's Prologue aloud. You could use an online audio version or the opening of a film or performance. Explain that this prologue comes before the play begins. What does Shakespeare tell us here about how the tragedy will end? Ask students to identify which elements of the tragedy we have witnessed already and what we learn from Shakespeare's Prologue about what is to come. Does it affect our enjoyment that the tale is so famous that we know the inevitable ending?

- Distribute **Worksheet 9.5.2** and display **PowerPoint slide 4** to help students visually identify with reworkings of the play.

Trying it yourself

- Read the information for the narrative task on the worksheet to clarify it for students, exploring 'The key ingredients' list and perhaps relating this back to events and ideas they have witnessed in the play. Allow time for students to plan their recasting using the five-point narrative plan on the worksheet. Encourage students to share their ideas with a partner to see if there is anything they could add or change to improve their plan.

Final task

- Allow time for students to complete the writing of their short story. This could include homework time to ensure successful and developed outcomes.

Taking it further

- Follow up on this with a reciprocal reading lesson of the remainder of Act 4, pages 201 to 219 *Collins Classroom Classics* edition.

Worksheet 9.5.2 — 'Shall I be married, then, to-morrow morning?'

The tragedy of Romeo and Juliet has been reworked many times and in many different forms. The musical *West Side Story* features two rival gangs and is set in New York in the 1950s. Malorie Blackman's novel *Noughts and Crosses* is set in an alternative society with two races: the Noughts and the Crosses. Both deal with the consequences of love against these backdrops and rivalries.

Activity

Plan and write a complete short story that features some or all of the key ingredients from the tragedy of *Romeo and Juliet*, listed in the box below. Think back to the diagram you used in Week 5, Lesson 2 of Year 8, as shown below.

- You can choose to set the story in any time period or location.
- You can create the characters of your young lovers in any way you wish: they could be from rival parts of town; different races, religions, or cultures; you could create characters who identify as LGBTQ+.
- You need to think of what the complication is that stands in their way.
- Consider what the climax of your story will be.
- What desperate choice will your central characters (or one character) have to make?
- How will your story end? What will be your moral, message, or intention?

The key ingredients

- A forbidden young love
- Fate
- Family honour
- Social conventions
- A violent society
- Rivalry
- Hasty actions
- Desperate choices

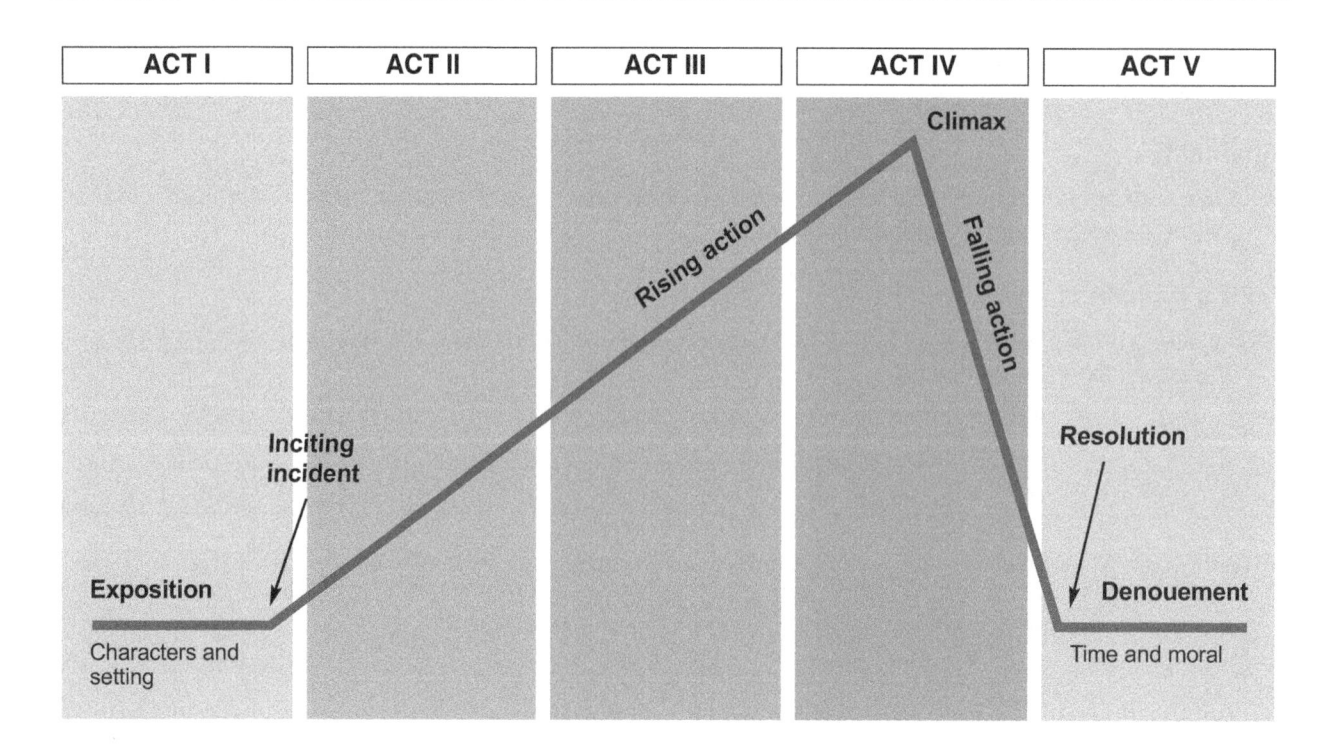

Story structure diagram

ACT I — Exposition (Characters and setting)
ACT II — Inciting incident, Rising action
ACT III — Rising action
ACT IV — Climax, Falling action
ACT V — Resolution, Denouement (Time and moral)

Extract 9.6.1
Act 5 Sc 1; Sc 3 — *'... I defy you, stars.'*

The story continues ...

Juliet returns from visiting the Friar and deceives her father into thinking she will marry Paris. A delighted Capulet brings forward the wedding by another day. On the eve of the wedding, Juliet asks to be left alone and drinks the potion. Early the next morning Paris arrives and the Nurse is sent to wake Juliet. The household are overcome with grief. Friar Lawrence comes, pretending to be arriving for the wedding, and arranges for Juliet's body to be taken to the Capulet tomb. Meanwhile, in Mantua, Romeo is unaware of the plan. His friend Balthasar has rushed to Mantua after hearing of Juliet's supposed death.

Extract 1, Act 5 Scene 1

[Enter BALTHASAR, Romeo's man.]

Romeo
News from Verona! How now, Balthasar!
Dost thou not bring me letters from the friar?
How doth my lady? Is my father well?
How fares my Juliet? That I ask again, 15
For nothing can be ill, if she be well.

Balthasar
Then she is well, and nothing can be ill.
Her body sleeps in Capels' monument,
And her immortal part with angels lives.
I saw her laid low in her kindred's vault, 20
And presently **took post** to tell it you.
O, pardon me for bringing these ill news,
Since you did leave it for my office, sir.

Romeo
Is it e'en so? Then I defy you, stars.
Thou knowest my lodging: get me ink and paper, 25
And hire post-horses; I will hence to-night.

Balthasar
I do beseech you, sir, have patience;
Your looks are pale and wild, and do import
Some misadventure.

Romeo
                    Tush, thou art deceiv'd;
Leave me, and do the thing I bid thee do. 30
Hast thou no letters to me from the friar?

Balthasar
No, my good lord.

Romeo

                                                           No matter; get thee gone,
And hire those horses; I'll be with thee straight.

[Exit BALTHASAR.]

Well, Juliet, I will lie with thee to-night.
Let's see for means. O mischief, thou art swift   35
To enter in the thoughts of desperate men!

Glossary

took post: hired a horse

The story continues ...

Romeo hurries back to Verona and arrives that night, after finding a poor apothecary who agrees to sell him a deadly poison. Friar Lawrence learns that his letter has not reached Mantua and rushes to the tomb in panic. Romeo, however, has reached the tomb first and finds Paris, who has come to lay flowers for Juliet. Romeo and Paris fight and Romeo, not realising who he is, kills him in desperation.

Extract 2, Act 5 Scene 3

[FRIAR LAWRENCE enters the tomb.]

Romeo! O, pale! Who else? What, Paris too?
And steep'd in blood? Ah, what an unkind hour   145
Is guilty of this lamentable chance!
The lady stirs.

[JULIET wakes.]

Juliet

O comfortable friar! Where is my lord?
I do remember well where I should be,
And there I am. Where is my Romeo?   150

[Noise within.]

Friar Lawrence

I hear some noise. Lady, come from that nest
Of death, contagion, and unnatural sleep;
A greater power than we can contradict
Hath thwarted our intents. Come, come away;
Thy husband in thy bosom there lies dead;   155
And Paris too. Come, I'll dispose of thee
Among a sisterhood of holy nuns.
Stay not to question, for the watch is coming;
Come, go, good Juliet. I dare no longer stay.

Juliet
>Go, get thee hence, for I will not away. 160

>>[*Exit* FRIAR LAWRENCE.]

>What's here? A cup, clos'd in my true love's hand?
>Poison, I see, hath been his timeless end.
>O churl! drunk all, and left no friendly drop
>To help me after? I will kiss thy lips;
>Haply some poison yet doth hang on them, 165
>To make me die with a restorative.
>Thy lips are warm.

>>[*Kisses him.*]

First Watch
>[*Within*]　　　　　　　　Lead, boy. Which way?

Juliet
>Yea, noise? Then I'll be brief. O happy dagger!

>>[*Snatching* ROMEO's *dagger.*]

>This is thy sheath; there rust, and let me die.

>>[*She stabs herself and falls on* ROMEO's *body.*]

Lesson 9.6.1 '... I defy you, stars.'

Learning objective(s):
- To understand the tragic conclusion to the play.
- To make connections from a key extract with the whole text.

Resources:
- PowerPoint 9.6.1
- Extract 9.6.1
- Worksheet 9.6.1

Getting started

- Share the lesson objectives on **PowerPoint slide 1** with the class. Display **PowerPoint slide 2** and ask students to predict what Romeo has discovered here. How do they interpret his response from the image? What might he be feeling?

- Distribute **Extract 9.6.1** and read aloud **The story continues ...**. Appoint two students to read **Extract 1, Act 5 Scene 1** aloud. Explore with students what Romeo means when he says: '... I defy you, stars.' How does this link back to his fears in Act 1 before Capulet's party?

Trying it yourself

- Distribute **Worksheet 9.6.1** and ask students to work individually on **Activity 1** to consolidate understanding. Aim for all students to use the clear comprehension method. Students should identify: *1. How Romeo was excited at the sight of Balthasar who he hoped was bringing news of Juliet; 2. How Balthasar has acted too hastily and brought a miscommunication to Romeo; 3. Romeo reacts equally hastily and with passion, as we have seen earlier in the play on meeting Juliet and in response to Mercutio's death; 4. Balthasar fears that Romeo is about to do something risky or dangerous for his own safety; 5. Romeo implies that he will be with Juliet in death.*

- Read aloud **The story continues ...** following **Extract 1**.

- To aid comprehension, read aloud or listen to an online audio version of Romeo's final speech at the Capulet tomb on **Worksheet 9.6.1**. Ask students to work in pairs or small groups on the speech, completing **Activity 2**. *In sequence, key images or motifs students should identify are: marriage; fate; death; light; humour in death; lightning; family honour/feud; the stars/ill fate.* Students might make several links and connections across the play. *Possible ideas include: Paris's suit with Capulet; Romeo's ill feeling before the Capulet feast; Juliet's words as Romeo left after their wedding night; Romeo's words in the Capulet orchard; Mercutio's reference to being 'a grave man'; Juliet's fear that their love was too much like lightning; Romeo's attempt to recognise Tybalt as family in Act 3; Romeo's numerous references to fate and the stars; the lovers' first kiss at the Capulet feast.*

- Appoint two more students to read aloud **Extract 2, Act 5 Scene 3**. Then, working with the whole class, use the prompts on **PowerPoint slide 3** to explore students' thoughts, feelings and reactions about the Friar at this point. Consider the option he gives Juliet of placing her in a nunnery and his own possible cowardice at being complicit in the secret marriage and deception. Ensure that students note how she changes from waking to see him as her 'comfortable Friar' to the sharp imperative of her final words to him: 'Go get thee hence, for I will not away.'

- If time is available, aim to watch a film clip or live production of Act 5 in its entirety with students before displaying **PowerPoint slide 4**.

Taking it further

- Use the final speeches from both fathers on **PowerPoint slide 4** as a final task for this lesson. Aim to question students about how the two characters respond to each other. What is interesting about what Montague calls Juliet ('true and faithful')? Might they have felt the same way if the secret marriage had come to light earlier? (Make sure students understand that 'enmity' means opposition or hostility.) What message do students feel Shakespeare is giving us here about parental control; about patriarchal rules; about family honour? Is he also giving a message about deception; the hasty actions of the young; not listening to parents or being honest with them? Where do students' sympathies lie the most?

Worksheet 9.6.1 '... I defy you, stars.'

Activity 1

Answer the following questions using the clear comprehension method:

- Make a clear statement addressing the focus of the question.
- Support it with a quotation from the extract.
- Show your understanding by making an inference.

1. What does Romeo assume in his first speech?
2. What mistake has Balthasar made?
3. How does Romeo react and what side of his character does this show?
4. What is Balthasar's fear when he sees Romeo's reaction?
5. What are Romeo's thoughts in his final speech of the extract?

Activity 2

Working together, read Romeo's final speech below. For each of the highlighted sections decide:

- What key image or motif from earlier in the play does Romeo use here?
- Think back over your work on the whole play and select a quotation from elsewhere in the play that directly connects with the highlighted quotation. Who says it and where?
- Add your notes and quotations as annotations to the speech.

Romeo

In faith, I will. Let me peruse this face.
Mercutio's kinsman, noble County Paris! 75
What said my man, when my betossed soul
Did not attend him as we rode? I think
He told me Paris should have married Juliet.
Said he not so, or did I dream it so?
Or am I mad, hearing him talk of Juliet, 80
To think it was so? O, give me thy hand,
One writ with me in sour misfortune's book!
I'll bury thee in a triumphant grave.
A grave? O no! a lantern, slaughter'd youth;
For here lies Juliet, and her beauty makes 85
This vault a feasting presence full of light.
Death, lie thou there, by a dead man interr'd.

[Laying PARIS in the tomb]

How oft when men are at the point of death
Have they been merry! Which their keepers call
A lightning before death. O, how may I 90
Call this a lightning? O my love! my wife!

Death, that hath suck'd the honey of thy breath,
Hath had no power yet upon thy beauty.
Thou art not conquer'd; beauty's ensign yet
Is crimson in thy lips and in thy cheeks, 95
And death's pale flag is not advanced there.
Tybalt, liest thou there in thy bloody sheet?
O, what more favour can I do to thee,
Than with that hand that cut thy youth in twain
To sunder his that was thine enemy? 100
Forgive me, cousin! Ah, dear Juliet,
Why art thou yet so fair? Shall I believe
That unsubstantial Death is amorous,
And that the lean abhorred monster keeps
Thee here in dark to be his paramour? 105
For fear of that I still will stay with thee,
And never from this palace of dim night
Depart again. Here, here will I remain
With worms that are thy chambermaids; O, here
Will I set up my everlasting rest, 110
And shake the yoke of inauspicious stars
From this world-wearied flesh. Eyes, look your last.
Arms, take your last embrace. And, lips, O you
The doors of breath, seal with a righteous kiss
A dateless bargain to engrossing death! 115
Come, bitter conduct, come, unsavoury guide.
Thou desperate pilot, now at once run on
The dashing rocks thy sea-sick weary bark.
Here's to my love! *[Drinks]* O true apothecary!
Thy drugs are quick. Thus with a kiss I die. *[Falls]* 120

Lesson 9.6.2 — 'See what a scourge is laid upon your hate'

Learning objective(s):
- To work as a team to produce a script for a documentary exploring one of the key ideas from Shakespeare's play in a modern context.

Resources:
- PowerPoint 9.6.2
- Worksheet 9.6.2

Recap and reflection

- Share the lesson objectives on **PowerPoint slide 1** with the class. Display **PowerPoint slide 2** and reflect on the prologue from the start of the play, which gives an overview of the whole plot. Ask students to reflect on whether they feel the play still has any relevance today or whether they feel it is too far removed from their own experiences. Which aspects of the prologue would they select as still having relevance today? Ask for specific words and phrases.

- Display **PowerPoint slides 3–5** in sequence, considering the images with students, along with the prompt questions and the linked quotations. Take different points of view from students in relation to each image and question. Encourage students to be sensitive, respectful and considerate in sharing their views. Explore the idea that even though the play was written over 400 years ago, we often consider Shakespeare's themes to be universal and to reflect unchanging aspects of human experience.

Final task

- Distribute **Worksheet 9.6.2**. Organise students into small groups and allow them to select their topic. Spend some time unpacking the task, which is designed to help them see the themes of the play in a modern context, using the help and prompts on the worksheet. Ask students to keep in mind the viewpoints shared in the preceding activity. Allow preparation time, which could include the opportunity for students to do some research and then plan their approach to their segment of the documentary.

- Encourage students to write individual point of view pieces to be delivered, interspersed with interviews and role play. Encourage them to think about how they will 'stitch' the different elements of their five-minute segment together, showing their knowledge, understanding and point of view in relation to their chosen topic. Allow time for the writing and sequencing of their different elements, checking content and helping with ideas.

- Allow some rehearsal time for piecing together their group outcomes.

- If time allows, this could stretch over two lessons to allow for the content and rehearsal to be perfected. If facilities allow, the documentary segments could be filmed.

Worksheet 9.6.2: 'See what a scourge is laid upon your hate'

You are working on a new documentary series aimed at young people, exploring the relevance of Shakespeare's plays and his universal themes today. Your team is working on an episode based on *Romeo and Juliet*.

Activity

Working in a small group, you are going to write and present a five-minute script that explores *one* of the following options:

- the relationships between parents and adolescents
- the risks to young people created by violence, feuds, or gangs
- the restrictions placed on some young people in terms of love and marriage.

You should:

- Link your chosen topic to its presentation in the play.
- Consider why the topic is still an issue today. Has it changed? Has it stayed the same?
- Make some conclusions as to Shakespeare's relevance today and what we can learn from our study of his work.

You will need to:

- Spend some time researching and gathering ideas for your chosen topic.
- Decide how you can link key elements of the play, its plot, themes and characters into your final piece.
- Decide on a range of interesting points of view that are sensitive, compassionate, balanced and inclusive without making judgments.
- Think about the sequence for your script, how you will introduce your segment of the programme and how it will end.
- Think about how you will present your work as a team.

You could:

- Use role play, interviews or a question-and-answer session as part of your work.
- Appoint an anchor person or persons to be your main presenter(s).

Acknowledgements

Every effort has been made to trace copyright holders and to obtain their permission for the use of copyright materials. The publishers will gladly receive any information enabling them to rectify any error or omission at the first opportunity.

Images

We are grateful to the following for permission to reproduce their images:

Cover Reading Room 2020 / Alamy Stock Photo

Year 7 PPT.7.1.1: Slide 2 Nsit/Shutterstock, PPT.7.2.1: Slide 3t WUT.ANUNAI/Shutterstock, PPT.7.2.1: Slide 3bl Fer Gregory/Shutterstock, PPT.7.2.1: Slide 3br Sebastian Janicki/Shutterstock, PPT.7.2.2: Slide 3l Atelier Sommerland/Shutterstock, PPT.7.2.2: Slide 3r Atelier Sommerland/Shutterstock, PPT.7.3.2: Slide 3 incamerastock / Alamy Stock Photo, PPT.7.3.2: Slide 5 vizizebra/Shutterstock, PPT.7.4.1: Slide 2 X3A Collection / Alamy Stock Photo, PPT.7.4.2: Slide 6 Michael D Brown/Shutterstock, PPT.7.5.1: Slide 4 HELGA NEVA/Shutterstock, PPT.7.5.2: Slide 2 Melkor3D/Shutterstock, PPT.7.5.2: Slide 3 Melkor3D/Shutterstock, PPT.7.6.1: Slide 4l Igor Sirbu/Shutterstock, PPT.7.6.1: Slide 4r SingerGM/Shutterstock, PPT.7.6.1: Slide 5l Asianet-Pakistan/Shutterstock, PPT.7.6.1: Slide 5r myboys.me/Shutterstock, PPT.7.6.1: Slide 6l Sepp photography/Shutterstock, PPT.7.6.1: Slide 6r DisobeyArt/Shutterstock, PPT.7.6.2: Slide 2 Liv Oeian/Shutterstock, WS.7.4.2 Michael D Brown/Shutterstock, WS.7.5.1 Tatiana Goncharuk/Shutterstock, WS.7.6.1l Igor Sirbu/Shutterstock, WS.7.6.1r SingerGM/Shutterstock

Year 8 PPT.8.1.1: Slide 2l Rudy Balasko/Shutterstock, PPT.8.1.1: Slide 3 Antiqua Print Gallery / Alamy Stock Photo, PPT.8.1.1: Slide 5 Classic Image / Alamy Stock Photo, PPT.8.1.2: Slide 2 Michelle Bridges / Alamy Stock Photo, PPT.8.1.2: Slide 3 Erta/Shutterstock, PPT.8.3.1: Slide 3 Everett Collection/Shutterstock, PPT.8.3.1: Slide 4tl Gentian Polovina/Shutterstock, PPT.8.3.1: Slide 4tr Tomas Marek/Shutterstock, PPT.8.3.1: Slide 4bl canebisca/Shutterstock, PPT.8.3.1: Slide 4br Pajor Pawel/Shutterstock, PPT.8.3.2: Slide 2 Vibrant Pictures / Alamy Stock Photo, PPT.8.3.2: Slide 5 JOAT/Shutterstock, PPT.8.3.2: Slide 6 Michelle Bridges / Alamy Stock Photo, PPT.8.4.1: Slide 2 Vibrant Pictures / Alamy Stock Photo, PPT.8.5.1: Slide 5 Donald Cooper / Alamy Stock Photo, PPT.8.6.1: Slide 4 Chronicle / Alamy Stock Photo, WS.8.2.1 Tanya Antusenok/Shutterstock, WS.8.2.2 Giuseppe_R/Shutterstock

Year 9 PPT.9.1.2: Slide 2 Lanmas / Alamy Stock Photo, PPT.9.2.1: Slide 2 vovan/Shutterstock, PPT.9.2.1: Slide 4 rawf8/Shutterstock, PPT.9.2.2: Slide 3 colaimages / Alamy Stock Photo, PPT.9.4.1: Slide 2 Donald Cooper / Alamy Stock Photo, PPT.9.4.1: Slide 2 Lina Truman/Shutterstock, PPT.9.5.2: Slide 4l BFA / Alamy Stock Photo, PPT.9.5.2: Slide 4r urbanbuzz / Alamy Stock Photo, PPT.9.6.1: Slide 2 Photo 12 / Alamy Stock Photo, PPT.9.6.2: Slide 3 Air Images/Shutterstock, PPT.9.6.2: Slide 4 Orangedrink/Shutterstock, PPT.9.6.2: Slide 5 Africa Studio/Shutterstock, WS.9.2.2 Kakosha/Shutterstock